D0885176

DEEP
CALLETH
DEEP

In Search of
Spiritual Authority by
RICHARD GAZOWSKY

ISBN 0-926629-10-7
Printed in Hong Kong

TABLE OF CONTENTS

FOREWORD

As we enter the last decade of this millenium God is raising up many voices, from many different backgrounds, to build His kingdom. Richard Gazowsky is one of them. Here's a man who enjoys what he's doing, regardless of the danger involved. He writes with a difference, a freshness, a flair that you seldom find among Christian writers. This book will keep you turning the pages just to find out what's next. It's exciting!

Jamie Buckingham
Editor-at-large
Charisma magazine

LUST OF THE HOLY GHOST

CHAPTER 1
ARRESTED IN CHINA

The Chinese interrogator's words cut like a buzz saw through my thoughts of self-defense. She reached into my tennis bag, and pulled out a stack of Chinese Bibles. "If these are yours, then read them to me!"

Her statement hung like a bad smell in the plain, dimly-lit room near the Canton border station. She stood barely 5 feet in height but a steely stare emanated from her that would cause even the tallest man to fidget. I was so nervous that my upper lip began to tremble uncontrollably. I knew it was dangerous to try to sneak Bibles across the border because just a month earlier thousands of students had been slaughtered at Tiananmen Square, in their quest for democracy and freedom of press. Something had driven me to put my very existence on the line and it surely wasn't the lack of excitement in my life.

Here I was, pastor of the largest Protestant church in San Francisco, married and father of three children, and with every excuse why I shouldn't be in a situation like this. But a force greater than my ability to reason had taken control of me two days earlier, when I was in the office of a Christian outreach which runs an operation smuggling Bibles behind the Bamboo Curtain.

A few years earlier a sweet little Chinese lady was busted for helping to smuggle one million Bibles by boat into Communist China, and recently eleven Christians had been arrested for witnessing in China.

I looked across our friend's humble office and saw a young New Zealander load up a stack of Bibles and head for one of eighteen border crossings. The brother in the office calmly commented, "See that young man there? He's responsible for more Bibles going across the border in two years than any person I know." Suddenly something deep within me called out that I, too, must put my Christianity on the line!

By now the Chinese interrogator had finished counting my Bibles.

"Fifty," she exclaimed in broken English. "Are these all for yourself, or are they for friends?"

"No, they're for friends."

"What are their addresses?"

"Well, I don't know their addresses. I mean, they are really mine. I was just planning on giving them away."

By now my mouth was quivering so badly I didn't know what to say. I couldn't just tell her that I was trying to smuggle them in. But then, wasn't it obvious? What was the punishment for smugglers? Whatever it was, I knew I was in trouble.

Then the thought hit me. This lady really doesn't know whether I speak other languages. I decided I might as well pray in tongues and ask God for an answer. Upon raising my hands the Holy Ghost fell on me and I began to pray in other tongues as the Spirit of God gave me utterance, right before her. As I continued to pray I noticed someone laughing in the room. I opened my eyes to see who it was. There was the stern-faced interrogator laughing uncontrollably. I stopped and looked at her in amazement. She held her hand to her face still giggling, reached down and grabbed two Bibles, shoved them into my hands and said, "Here, hide them and get going."

At this, I needed no further explanation. I quickly slipped the Bibles under my jacket and bolted to the exit. My friend Scot Elia was waiting for me just outside Customs with a ghostly look upon his face, for he had been there at the moment of my arrest. I quickly told him about the miracle as we rushed to take a taxi to the White Swan Hotel in Canton.

The next day we hired an English-speaking guide and set out on bicycles to tour the city streets. For a lunch location our guide chose a five-story Communist government-run restaurant. Each floor of the establishment was packed full of people eating at large round tables that could easily seat fifteen people. There were between thirty and forty waiters serving on each floor. We were eating on the fourth level. We had just finished our lunch and were casually talking with our guide when a petite young Chinese girl approached me, bowed, and said haltingly,

"Sir, have you brought a Bible for me?"

I turned to my guide as he questioned her in Chinese. Then, turning to me he said, "She seems to think you have brought a Bible for her."

Tears started welling up in my eyes, for I now knew the reason why the interrogator had given me the two Bibles.

"Not only do I have one, but I have two for you."

Her eyes lit up at the sight of the two Bibles. She quickly took them and bowed two or three times to express her thanks, and then scurried across the room to where a group of waitresses was standing. Upon reaching them she briefly opened up the Bible and she must have read some passages because a reverent silence fell upon the group. Scot and I looked at each other and began praising God that we had been able to be used by Him to deliver such an important gift of life to such deserving people.

WHY "LUST" OF THE HOLY GHOST?

Later, back at the White Swan Hotel, I began to contemplate what it was that drove me to jeopardize my life and what caused even greater men to make more demanding sacrifices. The Lord gave me this Scripture:

"For the flesh lusts against the Spirit, and the Spirit against the flesh; and these are contrary to one another, so that you do not do the things that you wish."[1]

Just as your flesh lusts against the Spirit so there is a "lust" of the Spirit that wars against your flesh. God showed me that it was this driving force that caused others and me to give our lives completely to Him.

Lust is a very powerful motivator. Think of the young man who, in the face of the fear of rejection and laughter of his friends, will walk across the room and introduce himself to a young girl that he admires. Sometimes that young man will be so nervous that he can barely talk. Yet something deep within him compels him to do so. No wonder Solomon said, "There are three things which are too wonderful for me...the way of a man with a virgin."[2]

DEEP CALLETH DEEP

It is in this same manner that the Spirit can lust against the flesh. God puts a driving call deep within you that will cause you to go

[1]Galatians 5:17
[2]Proverbs 30:18,19

through embarrassment before family and friends, fearing their rejection, to enable you to do the will of God. David said, "Deep calls unto deep."[3]

Skin divers refer to this as "rapture of the deep." I am told that something happens to skin divers when they reach certain depths of the ocean. Suddenly the hidden depths begin to call them to come deeper and, at this point, they have to force themselves to go to the top.

As a young man growing up I experienced "deep calling unto deep" in a different way. When I was six years old I acquired a craving for lemons. I would sneak into our family's icebox and would eat ten to fifteen of them at a sitting. When my mother went shopping I would beg her to buy more lemons and before we got home I would have already downed a few.

By the time I was nine my yearning for lemons had not abated. My parents were afraid I was going to ruin my teeth so they took me to the family doctor and asked him

---

[3]Psalm 42:7

what was wrong. After examining me he told them the problem was that deep within my young body there was a craving for certain vitamins that could only be satisfied by eating lemons. He advised my parents to begin giving me vitamin C pills.

As soon as I began taking the tablets my craving for lemons miraculously quit. This example shows how God puts an inner tug for His will deep within your spirit. It might be hard many times to explain to others why we Christians will do things that do not seem rational. But logical or not, I hope to explain in this book how to identify and yield to this inner call.

Many women have felt during pregnancy a sudden longing for some unusual food. Doctors explain this craving as being the child's hunger communicated deep within a woman, causing her to desire that particular nourishment. There are things that God is wanting to do with you, new dreams and visions waiting to be birthed, and you must prepare your heart to yield to these spiritual desires.

GOING BAREFOOT

When Moses stood before God the LORD told him, "Take your sandals off your feet."[4]

When Joshua stood before the commander of the LORD'S army the angel said, "Take your sandal off your foot."[5]

When David marched out of Jerusalem in defeat, running from his son Absalom, the Scripture tells us that he went up to the Mount of Olives "barefoot."[6]

When Boaz was negotiating for the hand of Ruth in marriage, he gave his sandal to his relative as a sign of covenant before the elders of Israel.[7]

As Boaz walked back through the town, he was saying to the men of that city that if he did not keep his commitment in marrying Ruth he would become the servant of his relative, for in Biblical times all of the

[4]Exodus 3:5
[5]Joshua 5:15
[6]2Samuel 15:30
[7]Ruth 4:7-8

servants walked barefoot while their masters wore shoes.

In each one of the examples above we see men who were leaders humbling themselves before God by taking the role of a servant and going barefoot. To all others this may seem foolish, but you will never do great things for God if you do not first understand and apply this principle to your personal life.

Something that each one of us, especially those who are Americans, has deeply ingrained within our flesh is: The protection of our rights. We must understand that when we make Jesus Christ Lord of our life, we are giving over our rights to Him. It is His responsibility to defend us, protect us, and provide for us.

While I was in Africa a missionary explained to me the blessings of "servanthood." In his house, upon his own bed, lay a very sick man with malaria. I asked him how long the man had been in that condition and he told me it had been a few weeks. He then explained to me that this man was a servant and had worked around his house for years. He told me, in that part of Africa, a servant's master was responsible for every aspect of his life, including health. If his house was leaking the servant simply was to go to his master and tell him he needed a new roof. The master would not reply, "I will take it out of your paycheck," as some of our bosses might say, but instead he would repair his roof.

As this missionary spoke, my mind was enlightened about our relationship with Jesus. When we make Jesus our Lord, we are getting a true "good Master" who will supply every need that we have. Did not Jesus say, "But seek first the kingdom of God and His righteousness, and all these things shall be added unto you"?[8]

Many of us who are seeking this deeper call, rather than mediocrity, will be misunderstood by our friends and relatives, even sometimes by those in the church. Remember Judas and his response to Mary's action of anointing Jesus' feet with the

---

[8]Matthew 6:33

"Look, I'm Judas. Would I lie? Of course they work. Ask Peter."

precious ointment: "Why was this fragrant oil wasted?"[9] He chided Jesus.

Consider how the world looks at waste as ~something which does not yield an immediate return to the giver. In other words, don't do something that does not satisfy or reward "self."

Let's take another look at what Judas was telling Jesus. "For it might have been sold for more than three hundred denarii and given to the poor."[10] Notice that Judas never did call Jesus "Lord." So really the question he was asking was, "Haven't you put this substance to the wrong use?" To Judas, she was not anointing the feet of God in preparation for burial, but instead she was making an extravagant display of affection. In other words, she was just satisfying Jesus' ego.

The world will question you in the same manner when you "just" satisfy the Lord and His desires. But isn't it about time we did

---

[9]Mark 14:4
[10]Mark 14:5

so? Let's seek the praises of God and not the praises of men!

For a moment, think about your prayer time. Do you pray until you're satisfied, or until God is satisfied? When you fulfill God's needs the whole house will be "filled with the fragrance of the oil."[11]

SET YOUR HEART TO WIN

When God created you, He designed you for success. That's why as a child, unless you had an extremely negative upbringing, you were constantly daydreaming about impossible accomplishments.

The deep calling within your spirit is driving you to success.

~Demand success for you and your family.

~Force yourself to dream beyond the "facts."

~Join the competition.

---

[11]John 12:3

Christianity is fraught with complacency. You can do better than over 50% of all the Christians in the world by just working hard. You can beat another 40% by being honest and playing by God's rules, making integrity your basis for action. (For example: Some pastors build their churches by coercing saints from other churches to join them and calling that revival). To beat the last 10%, it's a dogfight! But read on and join the competition.

THE CURSE OF HAM
CHAPTER 2

Reverend Marilynn Gazowsky had just finished her sermon text, and my recording group, "The Redeemed", began singing a composition written especially for the sermon. Suddenly, to the shock and amazement of the entire church, our assistant pastor, Bro. Larry, walked up to the pulpit and interrupted the song yelling, "This church is backslidden!" Gesturing in my direction he continued, "And *that* young man is responsible. I am leaving this church and forming a new one. If anyone wishes to go with me and my family, come and follow me right now!" With that he promptly left the pulpit and went to his wife, (my sister), and said, "Let's go." As they walked out of the church he motioned to other families he obviously had previously contacted to follow him. In all, about twenty people abruptly left the church.

A thick cloud of confusion hung above the heads of the remaining congregation. Some thought it was a skit (for I had been known to do dramatic presentations in church) and since Larry did this in the middle of my song they thought it was part of the program. What he had done was so shocking, most people could not believe that it had happened.

Sister Marilynn, the pastor, was also trying to recover. She had just lost a son-in-law and her daughter. All she could do was stumble to the pulpit with her face full of tears. With hands outstretched, she cried aloud, "Church, this can't be. Please come and pray."

I fell to my knees by the piano bench, trying to dodge the questioning looks from many of the saints. As I knelt there, the realization of what had happened charged my brain. *Larry was my hero. What evil had possessed him that he would try to destroy*

the church that both he and I had labored for
so diligently?

Sister Marilynn, my mother, had started
the church in San Francisco when I was
eleven years old. Larry was one of the first
young men to join our congregation. At that
time he was stationed here in the military.
My mother had instantly recognized him as a
talented speaker and a young man with an
"anointing" on his life. In a few years he
married my sister. In my young eyes the sun
rose and set on Larry. At times I would
mimic his preaching style in front of my
mirror at home. He was the male role-model
that I needed.

As the years went by, Larry became our
assistant pastor and my mother made it no
secret that one day he would lead the church.
After this announcement was initially made I
began to notice a change in him. Suddenly
he began to think that since he was going to
be pastor "he" knew how he would run the
church. Every decision Sister Marilynn made
passed through his mental filter: "But I
would do it differently."

Satan knows that this is fertile ground for rebellion. He feeds discontentment to saints who are promised a promotion. This is why the Scripture says, "Godliness with contentment is great gain."[12] Might I emphasize, any time you are promised a promotion you must not allow yourself to be tormented with the "if I was doing it" syndrome.

Happily, after a few years Larry came to grips with the fact that being pastor was a long-term and not a short-term goal. But by then he was being bothered by another factor: His old buddy Richard was now becoming a shining star in the church and might pose serious competition. Many of his complaints about me were well-founded, as I had the concept of "winning the lost" at any cost and many times would try to railroad my ideas through. When these conflicts would arise, Sister Marilynn would become the peacemaker.

As our church grew, the need for a new building became apparent. We purchased an

_____

[12] I Timothy 6:6

entire block in San Francisco, which included a theater which seated 2,000. The cost of remodeling the sanctuary alone was nearly two hundred thousand dollars. Larry was not much interested in construction, so I became head of the remodeling project while he was over the finances.

To give you a balanced picture of the resulting conflict, I must be honest and tell you that I cannot manage money. I would become so obsessed with getting the project done that I would ignore very vital and important details. One day while we were building the stage I saw Larry stomping down the aisle towards our temporary office for a confrontational meeting about me. I knew I had made some mistakes in purchasing too much insulation but I thought, "I'm here working and he's at home sticking his nose in books."

This was a vital mistake on my part in not understanding other men's callings. I stood and watched him close the door behind him, then I angrily released the buckle of my nail belt, let it slam to the floor, and headed

towards the office to defend myself.
Suddenly the Holy Ghost whispered to me,
"Do you want Me to be your defense or do
you want to defend yourself?" I stopped,
turned and went back to my work, but inside
my chest wild mustangs were struggling to
escape. That whole day I was fraught with
the desire to defend myself, but the Lord
made me hold my tongue...

THE LIE

There is a lie that satan communicates to
most Christians who desire a promotion, or
long for spiritual authority in the church. It is
as follows:

The time that is most ripe for
advancement is when those in leadership (or
those in competition with you) sin. By
exposing their sin to others you increase your
image of self-righteousness, thereby showing
others your ability to lead and judge
righteously. Nothing could be further from
the truth! Let me explain.

The Bible tells us the story of Noah and his sons. After the flood, "Noah began to be a farmer, and he planted a vineyard. Then he drank of the wine and was drunk, and became uncovered in his tent. And Ham, the father of Canaan, saw the nakedness of his father, and told his two brothers outside."[13]

In modern terminology, Noah is the pastor of the church; Ham, Shem, and Japheth are the assistant pastors. The assistant pastor Ham walks into the pastor's office and finds him nude, drunk and disgracing the ministry. Well, the obvious thought runs through Ham's mind: "The pastor has sinned and I must expose it so I will surely be promoted. Then all men will know that I, Ham, have stood for righteousness." So, Ham gleefully runs to his fellow assistant pastors and "spills the beans" on Pastor Noah.

---

[13] Genesis 9:20-22

Ham's big scoop.

But he is shocked by the response of his brothers. They don't rejoice or gossip, but he sees instead the look of hurt on their faces that is birthed by a deep love for their father and pastor. They rush out and grab a blanket, then turning their backs toward their father's door, they walk backwards into the pastor's office. Without turning around they cover Pastor Noah's sin!

This action reveals to us one of the most powerful keys to gaining authority and promotion in the church of God. Cover the mistakes of leaders. If exposure comes, the hand of God, or those He uses who are in proper authority above the person, should act upon it.

I once pulled up at a stoplight and saw in the car next to me a brother from the church smoking a cigarette. I turned to the brother who was riding with me and he, too, carried the same amazed look on his face. When the light turned green I pulled the car over to the side of the road. We both began to go into intercession for our brother. He did not see us but drove on, not knowing what was transpiring in our car. We must have prayed for over 15 minutes before the burden for that man left us.

We didn't talk about his sin nor expose him to anyone . Instead, we placed him in the hands of God. Two weeks later that same brother confessed his deliverance from the sin he had been hiding for ten years! When God shows you another Christian's sin, He is not doing it so you can take advantage of that person's weakness, but so you can lift the burden of that sin from his shoulders.

This is what Shem and Japheth had done for their father Noah. When Noah awoke, I believe God revealed to him what his son Ham had done. Ham tried to take advantage of his father's weakness. Noah then pronounced this judgment to his son: "Cursed be Canaan; a servant of servants. He shall be to his brethren."[14] Noah then turned to his other two sons and said, "Blessed be the LORD, the God of Shem, and may Canaan be his servant. May God enlarge

---

[14] Genesis 9:25

Japheth, And may he dwell in the tents of Shem; And may Canaan be his servant."[15]

Here you can see how powerful this truth is: Instead of Ham receiving a promotion he was demoted to meniality. This is called by many Bible scholars "the curse of Ham."

REBELLION: THE CURSE OF HAM

Recently I was visiting a pastor friend who had been struggling for six years to build a church. He hadn't been able to get more than 25 people to consistently attend his congregation. Frustrated, he asked me to come and talk with him. Instead of presenting him with new methods of outreach, I felt the Holy Spirit prompt me to ask about his reasons for starting a church in the first place. He then related this sad tale.

He was a youth minister at a large church when he suspected that the assistant pastor might be cheating on his wife. He snuck

---

15 Ibid. 9:26-27

around and tried to confirm the rumor. When he found out the truth, he exposed the offending couple and marched them into the pastor's office like a hunter with two trophies. He also made sure as many people as possible in the church knew about the adultery. He made it almost impossible for this assistant pastor and his wife to make reconciliation, for most of the church knew about it before *she* did. The destruction this disclosure caused in the church made it difficult for the young man to stay on as a youth minister. This is why he decided to start a new church.

This young minister did not know he was suffering from the curse of Ham. For the Bible says, "You are inexcusable, O man, whoever you are who judge, for in whatever you judge another you condemn yourself; for you who judge practice the same things."[16] The message in this verse is very deep and is not understood by many Christians. The power of self-righteous judgment against another person is usually found in the judging person's *own* guilt.

---

[16] Romans 2:1

So it was with my young pastor friend. He had allowed a root of bitterness to defile him, which caused him to rebel against his brother rather than restore him. Paul told us, "If a man is overtaken in any trespass you who are spiritual restore such a one in a spirit of gentleness, considering yourself lest you also be tempted."[17]

You should never be concerned with exposing someone's weakness or sin to other Christians, but instead should be doing everything possible to see that the person is reestablished. Every time you share that person's failure with another Christian you make it more difficult for the person to be rehabilitated, and you weaken the faith of the Christian.

I told this young pastor that he must become a repairer of relationships and go back and see if he could offer to make right the wrongful situation that he helped foster. When he truly receives the ministry of restoration, he will see the fruits of growth in

---

[17] Galatians 6:1

his own church and will break "the curse of Ham."

BACK TO LARRY

This same curse of Ham began to infect Larry's spirit. Some of this was caused by the promise that he would soon be made pastor, thereby adding fuel to his fire to expose faults in me, his competitor, or in Sister Marilynn, his pastor. He obviously kept these feelings in check until he met the most dangerous thing that a person who is discontent can meet: A willing ear. This "willing ear" came in the form of a couple who also were longing for a promotion. They soon formed a conspiracy.

The outbursts that Larry gave that fateful night in church probably would have never happened if it had not been for a visit to Larry's house two weeks earlier by an older minister. This minister was highly respected and considered to be beyond reproach when it came to wisdom and counsel. After dinner was finished he turned to Larry while his wife (my sister) was cleaning the dishes. "You know, Larry, it's time you stood up to Sister Marilynn and let her know that you are the MAN in the church," the minister said.

(I must comment here, that you should be careful with the counsel you get from some "wise" old counselors. I have many times been misdirected by men because I respected them for their age alone. It is important that you also check out a man's life. What kind of a church does he pastor? Are his children saved? Sorry to say, this counsel which was given to Larry became a stamp of approval for the seeds of rebellion).

Larry did go out to start a church, which lasted for about a year and a half. Eventually he became plagued with the problem of alcoholism, couldn't hold a job, and in fear of her life my sister left him. Two months before I was installed as pastor of the Voice of Pentecost, Sister Marilynn's church, I preached Larry's funeral. In a last-ditch effort to end the turmoil of his soul he committed suicide and was found two days later in a rented motel room. He was buried in one of my suits for he had none of his own.

Relating this story is very difficult as I still have a deep sense of love for Larry. He was a good man who became infected by an ugly spirit. One of our ministers met with him a few weeks before he died and asked him, "Larry why don't you come back home?" He simply replied, "Pride." Rebellion is like a disease. Once you are infected, it manifests itself in many forms and symptoms. (A year after Larry's death, the Lord blessed my sister and she met, and later married, an understanding and loving man).

The main reason, I have found, that causes men to lose out with God and thereby forfeit spiritual authority, is rebellion. Remember: Any time you rebel, it is because you are *"right."* **But rebellion is wrong.**

DEFINING SPIRITUAL AUTHORITY

CHAPTER 3
THE FLOWERS FADE

Spiritual authority should not be confused with power~the ability to push others around. Instead, I am talking about the authority that commands respect in both the spiritual and physical worlds.

The sons of Sceva thought they could operate in the realm of spiritual authority. When they tried to cast a demon out of a possessed man the demon replied, "Jesus I know, and Paul I know; but who are you?"[18] The demon-possessed man then jumped upon

---

[18]Acts 19:15

them, tore their clothes off, and they ran from the house naked. You can act like you have authority and talk like you have authority but if you don't have it, satan can easily overtake you, batter you, rip your "clothes" of self-righteousness off and send you through the town naked and bruised.

As a matter of fact, this is happening to many of the large ministries today. They have built kingdoms which are not based on true spiritual authority. Many of these ministries are basking in the excitement of fleshly accomplishments, but the prophet Isaiah said, "All flesh is grass, and all its loveliness is like the flower of the field. The grass withers, the flower fades, because the breath of the LORD blows upon it; surely the people are grass."[19]

James repeats this in the New Testament: "Let the lowly brother glory in his exaltation, but the rich in his humiliation, because as a flower of the field he will pass away."[20]

---

[19]Isaiah 40:6-7
[20]James 1:10

Peter makes this subject even clearer when he wrote, "All flesh is as grass, and all the glory of man as the flower of the grass. The grass withers, and its flower falls away."[21]

These verses demonstrate that any ministry that is built upon the ability and talents of its leaders, and not on their true authority with God, must be destroyed by God because, "No flesh should glory in His presence."[22]

This is why in a church service a sermon is often judged by the audience's response and not by the presence and response of the Lord. If we are not careful, we will start a self-perpetuating system that encourages speakers and singers to be more entertaining than powerful (by "powerful" I also do not mean scary or negative). Any ministry that is based upon popularity, and where success is measured by mass-acceptance, is putting itself in a very precarious position because, if

---

[21] Peter 1:24
[22] Corinthians 1:29

"Did you hear the one about Moses and the hail?"

it is a fleshly ministry, God must cut the grass and let the flowers fade.

Flesh-dependent ministries must be cancelled. Moses was driven into the wilderness for forty years. His talents and abilities had undergone a great transformation. When he appeared before God, the five excuses he gave were really five talents he previously had while in Egypt. For example, he said, "I cannot speak"~but the song of Moses is one of the greatest speeches ever written. He said, "Who will believe me? I have no credibility"~but who would have more credence than the son of Pharaoh's daughter? God took every one of Moses' flimsy points and made Moses aware of his dependency upon God in each area. Did not Paul say, "When I am weak, then I am strong"?[23]

Recently at Fuller Theological Seminary this statement was made: "You can tell the thin, entertainment-based ministers by their comments, 'Now, *that* will preach', versus

---

[23]2 Corinthians 12:10

the ministers who are concerned with the Biblical health of the flock, who pray for them to spiritually and physically see the power of God work miracles in their personal lives." Many times when ministers say, "Now, *that* will preach," they are saying, "Give me a cute little angle on some old familiar Biblical story so I can get the people to shout by my cleverness of interpretation."

Well, I predict that these days are over and that the time is coming, and now is, when true saints and ministers are going to have to depend on the authority and power of God and not the cuteness of man.

ORDAINED AUTHORITY

Let's look at how Paul defines authority in the Book of Romans. "Let every soul be subject to the governing authorities. For there is no authority except from God, and the authorities that exist are appointed by God.

Therefore whoever resists the authority resists the ordinance of God, and those who resist will bring judgment on themselves.

For rulers are not a terror to good works, but to evil. Do you want to be unafraid of the authority? Do what is good, and you will have praise from the same.

For he is God's minister to you for good. But if you do evil, be afraid; for he does not bear the sword in vain; for he is God's minister, an avenger to execute wrath on him who practices evil.

Therefore you must be subject, not only because of wrath but also for conscience' sake.

For because of this you also pay taxes, for they are God's ministers attending continually to this very thing."[24]

I have had many people ask, "But does this mean we must be subject to sinners who are in authority?" Wait a minute, did you forget who this book was written to? Was it not to the Romans? And did not Paul refer to paying taxes? So, he obviously was not talking about just those in the church. He was talking about those in the Roman

---

[24] Romans 13:2-6

government. You may contend that their leaders weren't as bad as ours today. Then I will ask you, "Who could be worse than the man who was Emperor at the time when Paul wrote this letter?" His name was Nero and he was responsible for crucifying over 150,000 Christians. As a matter of fact, it was Nero who killed Paul.

I know some of you who are reading this may find the concept hard to grasp, but if you'll bear with me I will try to explain to you how these Scriptural principles work. You will also see that by being under submission to the authority above, you can be brought into perfect alignment with God's perfect authority.

To show you how spiritual authority works I must show you how it is neutralized. Your authority with God is nullified by the spirit of rebellion.

WITCHCRAFT

Samuel said, "Rebellion is as the sin of witchcraft"[25], which means that rebellion is

---

[25] 1 Samuel 15:23

equal to witchcraft. Witchcraft means to work enchantments upon someone, and enchantment is another word for control. To put it another way, rebellion places you under control of the spirit of satan even if you are rebelling for a righteous cause!

Let's consider Aaron and his sons. In Leviticus 8 and 9, we find Aaron and his sons bringing sacrifices before God, and in this capacity everything is fine. It is much like a pastor and his assistant pastors conducting services every week.

But then something strange happens. Two of the assistant pastors call for a special service when the pastor is not there. God is displeased so he destroys them. Though I told this in a modern framework, this is exactly what happened as recorded in the Book of Leviticus:

"Nadab and Abihu, the sons of Aaron, each took his censer and put fire in it, put incense on it, and offered profane fire before the LORD, **which He had not commanded them.** So fire went out from the LORD and devoured them, and they died before the Lord."[26]   It was OK for his two sons to minister before the Lord as long as they were doing it under their father's authority. But as soon as they did that which he had not commanded them to do, God consumed them. Rebellion is taking God's authority into your own hands.

Another example of this is found in the story of Miriam and Aaron. Miriam had a good excuse for getting angry at Moses, for he had just brought home another wife who was not even an Israelite. She was Ethiopian (such women are beautiful, which could also have had a play in Miriam's outburst).

Hadn't Moses said with his own mouth, "Let them marry whom they think best, but they may marry **only within the family of their father's tribe**"?[27]   Did not Moses commission the people with these words, "When the LORD your God brings you into the land which you go to possess...you shall make no covenant...**nor shall you make marriages with them**"?[28]   Miriam was

---

[26] Leviticus 10:1-2
[27] Numbers 36:6
[28] Deuteronomy 7:1,2,3

saying, "Look, Bud, if it is good for the goose it's good for the gander!"

Miriam's belief was Biblically correct. As long as she kept her opinion within the confines of her family tent she had a right to express it. For wasn't she the one who watched over baby Moses when he was hid in the bulrushes of Egypt? She went wrong when she took her view outside of the tent and attacked Moses' ability to lead the people of Israel and hear the voice of God. She thought Moses blew it, but that was not what God thought. Here we find a clear example of how God views authority.

Let's consider each person's reaction to this challenge of authority.

MOSES' RESPONSE

Moses responds humbly and does not condemn his sister's attack but instead asks Miriam and Aaron to go with him into the tabernacle and ask God His opinion (unlike many pastors or Christian leaders who,when they are attacked, respond just the opposite).

A young man in our church once came and condemned me for a decision I had made and said that it proved that I was arrogant and proud. I thought, *"Wow, what if what he is saying is true?"* I asked him to come with me to the prayer room and we would ask the Lord to reveal the source of this arrogance in my heart.

As we walked through the prayer room doors I was shocked to see this man fall on his face and weep bitterly as he begged God to forgive him for attacking me! He later told me that he had felt God's presence so strongly that he saw the true nature of his sin; that he had been secretly desiring my position for years! This is not necessarily proof that I do not have a problem with arrogance or pride, but I am saying that this man's rebellion was more important to God at that moment than any other problem that could have been present in me.

When I was publishing R&R Magazine I received a letter from a minister that said in plain and simple English that the magazine was an extension of my alter ego and it showed no glory to God but only to myself! The secretary who opened this letter was upset. She wanted to write a blistering letter to this man and tell him "a thing or two."

But when she shared the letter with me the Lord checked my spirit. What if the letter was true? What would it hurt for me to take the letter into the prayer room and ask God if this was His opinion?

Well, guess what? To my own shock and amazement, I discovered in the prayer room that the Lord agreed with the man in some of his statements. So, instead of writing a cutting reply I responded with a "thank you" letter. Best of all, this prayer session helped show me that the magazine was an unprofitable drain on our church's finances. After a few more events had transpired we were able to close the operation graciously and move on to a more effective ministry.

GOD'S RESPONSE

When Moses, Miriam, and Aaron walked into the presence of God, you'd have thought that God would have been upset with Moses, would have corrected him, and then dealt kindly with Miriam and Aaron. But instead, God gave Moses one of the greatest compliments he'd ever received when He said, "...He is faithful in all My house. I speak with him face to face. Why then were you not afraid to speak against my servant Moses?"[29]

By seeing God's response to the situation, we see another spiritual principle in operation. God is very jealous concerning judgment. Did not He say, "Vengeance is Mine, and recompense"?[30]

This cardinal rule was also clearly expressed by Solomon when he said, "Do not rejoice when your enemy falls, and do not let your heart be glad when he stumbles; lest the LORD see it, and it displease Him, and He turn away His wrath from him."[31] This Scripture shows us that God probably would have corrected him if Miriam and Aaron had not interfered. And, they

29 Numbers 12: 7-8,8
30 Deuteronomy 32:35
31 Proverbs 24:17-18

probably reaped some of Moses' own judgment!

Many times I feel saints who are under pastors who stumble and make mistakes, end up allowing their pastor undeserved protection from the judgment of God because of their rebellious heart in trying to take things into their own hands. Every time you seek to do evil to someone in authority over you, you really pluck them out of the hand of God's judgment thereby increasing your own frustration, because it looks like God is not doing anything or hearing your prayers. He isn't. Secondly, it stops this person in leadership from receiving the blessings of God's correction.

James warned us about the dangers of seeking to bring down judgment upon people when he said, "For the wrath of man does not produce the righteousness of God."[32] As a matter of fact, Jesus rebuked His disciples when they wanted to call fire down from heaven upon the Samaritans after they were kicked out of town and not given a place to

---

[32] James 1:20

stay. Jesus said, "You do not know what manner of spirit you are of."[33]

When rebellion comes on you, you feel so righteous that you honestly have a hard time discerning that the rebellion is an evil spirit. This is because rebellion is rooted in self-righteousness. Even if Miriam and Aaron were technically right, the spirit of rebellion tipped the scales of judgment upon themselves, and God judged them instead.

AARON'S RESPONSE

Aaron, as usual, hung loose and kept his mouth shut.

MIRIAM'S RESPONSE

She's the one who did all the talking and she's the one who got into the most trouble. Strutting into the temple, she probably expected God to jump on her bandwagon. Instead, she was ceremoniously cursed with leprosy from the top of her head to the soul of her feet. She became leprous, as white as snow.

---

[33] Luke 9:55

God taught Moses a great lesson at the burning bush about leprosy when He told him to reach his hand into his side. When Moses pulled it out, his hand was full of leprosy, showing a spiritual allegory. If you reach to yourself, you will receive corruption.

Leprosy was also a disease that resulted from pride and self-righteousness. King Uzziah, in the throes of pride, thought he was "hot" enough to go into the temple and offer incense upon the altar. As the priests tried to stop him the Scripture relates that leprosy appeared upon his forehead even as they talked with him. No wonder Isaiah said, "In the year that King Uzziah died, I saw the Lord sitting on a throne, high and lifted up, and the train of His robe filled the temple."[34]

Each one of us will have moments when we feel our complaints are justified, as Miriam did. But let us not forget her end.

---

[34] Isaiah 6:1

King Saul keeping rebellion under control.

REBELLION IS CATCHY

Any time a person rebels, they loose forth a spirit at their work, in church, at home or in school. And so it was in this incident with Miriam. Soon that same defiance grew into the rebellion of the sons of Korah, and ultimately resulted in the death of over 14,950 people. One group perished by the ground eating them up, and the other by plague. This is why Paul warned us, "Lest any root of bitterness springing up cause trouble, and by this many become defiled."[35]

I have seen a father come home angry at his boss, complaining about how he was unjustly treated at work, yet still not understand later why his teenage boy rebels against him and his leadership of the family. Rebellion is like a disease that breeds faster than cancer. If you are not careful, your self-righteous complaining can spell the destruction of your own happiness and security.

---

[35] Hebrews 12:15

OBEDIENCE

Did you ever wonder why Moses asked Pharaoh's permission for the people of Israel to leave Egypt and worship God? Why didn't Moses just take the people and go? Shouldn't he "obey God rather than man"? [36] After all, Pharaoh was a sinner! Let's look back at the Scripture we quoted earlier from Romans. It says, "For there is no authority except from God, and the authorities that exist are appointed by God."[37]

Moses understood this principle and because he did, God could greatly use him and the people of Israel to display His glory to a heathen nation. By Moses being obedient to Pharaoh's directive that he could not go, he submitted Pharaoh to the power of God. When you walk in obedience, you submit leadership to the judgment of God. This is why Paul, when writing to the Corinthian church concerning spiritual warfare, said, "Being ready to punish all

---

[36] Acts 5:29
[37] Romans 13:1

disobedience **when your obedience is fulfilled.**"[38]

David was one of the most beautiful examples of "obedience subduing disobedient leadership." David had been anointed "king" over Israel and had become extremely popular after killing Goliath and other numerous enemies of Israel. One day while he was at King Saul's palace, Saul, his leader and father-in-law, grabbed a javelin and threw it at David, barely missing him and driving the spear into the wall. David was a man of war. He could have easily grabbed the spear out of the wall and thrown it back at King Saul.

Have we not all had this temptation when a pastor, boss, or other leader cuts us down verbally in front of others? Haven't we felt the desire to send a searing remark right back in their direction? Well, David didn't retaliate. Instead, he went to the countryside with a bunch of vagabond soldiers and helped protect Saul's kingdom from attack. Saul's jealousy of David only increased, until

[38] 2 Corinthians10:6

he was chasing David throughout the countryside.

One night while Saul was on this campaign, David found the king sleeping in a cave. As they looked down on his sleeping body, David's men told him to kill Saul because it was obvious God had delivered the king into his hands. But David said, "Do not destroy him; for who can stretch out his hand against the LORD's anointed, and be guiltless?"[39] Instead, he took Saul's sword and cut a piece of his garment.

To show you how sensitive he was to spiritual authority, even this act of making King Saul look silly bothered David's conscience. We should be perceptive to those in leadership above us, even to areas where they are vulnerable, pledging not to take advantage of them. If they need judgment, let God do it.

One night before service in our church in San Francisco, a young minister came and said he would like to set up a meeting with me concerning the future of his ministry.

[39] 1 Samuel 26:9

The next day we met at a restaurant and he told me how his pastor had made a grave mistake in judgment. This young minister was ready to take thirty-five members from his fellowship and bring them to our church so they could live a more "holy life." I looked at him sternly across the table and asked, "Have you ever made a mistake ?"

"Why, of course," he replied.

"And what did your pastor do?"

"Well, I backslid once and he restored me back to the ministry."

"So, here is your pastor fighting in the foxholes of San Francisco trying to establish a church for the name of Jesus and suddenly, after fifty years of ministry, he's wounded. And how does his son in the gospel respond? He pulls out a gun, points it at his face and pulls the trigger. Is that what you call love? I'll have no part with your thirty-five people coming to my church. But I will help restore you back to fellowship with your pastor."

This pastor in question died about a year later, but thank God his relationship with the young man was restored. The road to power always lies in our obedience. Is not Jesus the ultimate example of this? Paul wrote, "Let this mind be in you which was also in Christ Jesus...He humbled himself and became obedient to the point of death."[40]

Paul also tells us that Jesus "...learned obedience by the things which He suffered. And having been perfected, He became the author of eternal salvation to all who obey Him."[41] This shows us that obedience can be a learned attribute, if you apply yourself.

For years I thought a great anointing was suddenly going to fall on me from Heaven, and at that point I would have great authority and power with God. But guess what? It never happened. I sat in church service upon church service waiting for that special anointing to drop out of the sky.

God has shown me that anointing comes through a process of developing a deep spiritual life through obedience and action. Peter told the Sanhedrin court, "We are His

---

40 Philippians 2:5,8
41 Hebrews 5:8-9

witnesses to these things, and so also is the Holy Spirit whom God hath given to those who obey Him."[42]

Obedience is something YOU do, and it will give you power. At one time I was planning on giving a presentation at a Christian conference of a denomination other than the one I am licensed with. I had invested nearly $20,000 dollars in a magazine project to be presented there. The week before it was to convene I received a call from an official of my own denomination. He asked me to cancel the trip and gave me some reasons why I should not fellowship with these other "brethren." I disagreed with his reasons but I cancelled the trip anyway, amid the strong protests of my staff. They argued, "But he's wrong, and we've invested too much money in this project. You've got to go. This is for the work of God!"

I didn't go, and because of this and other reasons I mentioned earlier, the magazine project eventually did fail. But later I was appointed to a powerful position of influence

---

[42] Acts 5:32

within my organization because of this incident of obedience.

In light of some of the truths I have been sharing with you, you can imagine my feelings when I received a book from one of America's leading evangelists, who had fallen into sin because of moral failure. Refusing to be in obedience to the prescribed restoration process, he left his denomination and formed one of his own. The book was entitled, "To Obey God Rather Than Man."

The book tries to establish the point that because the denomination's decision hurt the evangelist's ministry, their decision could not be of God and thereby should be disobeyed. What a dangerous position to hold! By taking this stance a person equates their own ministry with the will of God.

King Herod gave a speech to the people of Tyre and they attributed his "delivery" to divinity. They shouted, "...the voice of a god and not of a man. Then immediately an angel of the Lord struck him, because he did not give glory to God. And he was eaten by worms and died."[43]   There is no ministry that is so anointed that God cannot do without it.

My wife, Sandy, and I, over the past year, had been hosting a fifteen-minute broadcast on a large Northern California radio station. In our first year of being on the air we had received over 4,000 responses, and donations had already started coming in on a continual basis, without us making pleas on the radio. Suddenly one day, the Lord spoke to me and said, "I want you to stop the program and go off the air." God also gave me the Scripture, "Unless a grain of wheat falls into the ground and dies, it remains alone; but if it dies, it produces much grain."[44] When I broke the news to the radio station, the manager came over to see me.

"Richard, is this a message that we are not doing something right? Do you want us to charge you a lower rate?"

I told him that it had nothing to do with them. It was a matter of obeying the voice of God, and that was it! Isn't it funny that we

---

[43] Acts 12:22,23
[44] John 12:24

always feel it's the will of God to start something but we never feel it is God's will to stop? Consider how many ministries today are out there dead on the vine, just hanging around and not producing fruit. They are just going through the motions. Jesus said He prunes us so we can bring forth much more fruit. God, give us the ability not only to bear babies, but also to bury the dead.

I have been pastoring for nearly two years in San Francisco. One of my first projects was to cut out dead, non-productive ministries. For example, we had been going to certain convalescent hospitals for over 16 years, without one person being established in the Lord. I finally said, "Enough is enough." Do you think Peter, a fisherman by trade, would have come home day after day for 16 years with an empty boat, rejoicing because he cast his net upon the waters? Of course not! He would do what every fisherman does~find a better fishing hole. If you are ever going to gain spiritual authority you must make up your mind now to obey

God, whether or not it is profitable in your eyes.

LEGITIMATE AUTHORITY

The Bible defines the four structures of authority listed below:

1. **Your family.** This line of authority dates all the way back to Adam and Eve, when God set up Adam as head of the family. Numerous Scriptures support this, including one by Paul which states, "Children, obey your parents in all things, for this is well pleasing to the Lord."[45]

I have seen a lot of misunderstanding in this area, especially by women whose husbands are not serving God. Let me share an example with you .

One sister I know had an unsaved, but financially very well off and moderately considerate, husband. She loved him dearly and lived with him in harmony for many years after she was saved. But suddenly she began to fellowship with other sisters who

---

[45] Colossians 3:20

also had husbands who were not Christians. As these women began to share their horror stories about living with unsaved men, this sister began to think differently about her relationship with her husband.

Over a period of a year she began to develop the "him against me-and-God" attitude. Soon, she found it hard to really love him affectionately because he was "the enemy." As he began to experience less and less affection from her, satan saw his chance and sent the man's old girlfriend by. Starved for appreciation, he responded to her advances. Soon this sister was left with a divorce, mounting bills, children without a daddy and one big REAL horror story.

You must realize that only in obedience and with spiritual authority can you subdue that unsaved man of yours. Peter said, "Wives, be submissive to your own husbands, that even if some do not obey the word, they, without a word, may be won by the conduct of their wives."[46] What kind of

---

[46] 1 Peter 3:1

conduct do you think Peter was talking about?

Let me give you a hint. What if you, who has an unsaved husband, went on a fast and got so full of the Holy Ghost that you prayed all day long waiting for your man to come home. And, just before he arrived home, you fixed his favorite meal, dressed in your most attractive attire and loved him when he walked in the door instead of preaching at him. The Bible says that "...they shall become one flesh"[47], speaking of marriage.

We have always looked at this Scripture in a negative light, understanding that a believer should not marry an unbeliever. This is true. But what if you have already married an unbeliever? Well, I believe by you getting full of the Holy Ghost, he is going to be overcome by the power of God in you when you come together. You don't even have to say anything. He'll know that it's Jesus that makes the difference in your marriage.

---

[47] Genesis 2:24

Don't become part of the mate-bashing crowd, but respect this God-ordained line of authority.

2. **Your national government.** It is funny that on this point many Christians are unclear, but the Bible seems to be pretty "black and white" on this issue. As a matter of fact, some of the strongest language used in the New Testament is written by Peter on this subject. He wrote, "Those who walk according to the flesh in the lust of uncleanness and despise authority. They are presumptuous, self-willed; they are not afraid to speak evil of dignitaries, whereas angels, who are greater in power and might, do not bring a reviling accusation against them before the Lord.

But these, like natural brute beasts made to be caught and destroyed, speak of things they do not understand, and will utterly perish in their own corruption, and will receive the wages of unrighteousness".[48]

I can't tell you of the times I have been guilty of entering into conversations at work

---

[48] 2 Peter 2:10-13

or elsewhere, criticizing the government instead of submitting the government to God. What most of us don't understand is that even though the criticism may be accurate and upright, the spirit of judging is wrong and that spirit will affect every aspect of your life.

Countless evening meals have been ruined because dad is upset over what the president or some senator has done about some current issue and most likely it doesn't pertain to dad and never will. But one thing it did was, it gave his kids heartburn and nurtured the seeds of rebellion in their hearts.

3. **Your church family.** Paul asked us to, "Remember those who rule over you, who have spoken the word of God to you, whose faith follow."[49] If you have not submitted yourself to the authority of some local congregation, do so immediately! Countless Christians are wandering on a sea of self-will, not realizing they cannot function properly when they are out of the "body" of Christ. You can't stand back and say you

---

49 Hebrews 13:7

don't think the church is what it should be and therefore you don't have to take part; you can't keep running to the "more perfect" denomination, or independent crowd.

During the time of Elijah there were two denominations. Judah was the one with the anointing. They had the temple and the Levitical priesthood. Elijah was sent to the backslidden denomination, Israel. They worshipped Baal in idol groves on mountain tops and were backslidden in every way, from King Ahab on down. As a matter of fact, Elijah had a "congregation" of only 7,000 people in the entire nation, but can you tell me who the prophet sent to Judah was? His name is hardly known. But every Bible student knows Elijah and the great miracles done through him by God.

Stick with your denomination and bring the power of God to them. Stay at your church and let the Holy Spirit bring revelation of power to His people through you.

4. **Your place of work.** Paul instructed early Christians: "Servants, obey in all things your masters according to the

flesh, not with eyeservice, as men-pleasers, but in sincerity of heart, fearing God. And whatever you do, do it heartily, as to the Lord and not to men."[50]   Check out the exciting promise in this verse! He says you are not really working for your boss but for God, and He will reward you.

I need to warn you that there are illegitimate lines of authority that will try to get you to rebel against your workplace, such as unions. The only time a Christian should obey a union above a boss is when the union is signing the paycheck. Don't let shop stewards or any other person sew seeds of discontent into your heart.

Learn to be "content with your wages."[51] Remember, David said, "For exaltation comes neither from the east, nor from the west nor from the south. But God is the judge: He puts down one and exalts another."[52]   Put your trust in God for promotion at work. You will be shocked at

---

[50] Colossians 3:22,23
[51] Luke 3:14
[52] Psalm 75:6-7

how swiftly He can move you up the proverbial ladder.

AVOIDING DISOBEDIENCE

I would like to share with you some common steps that people take when tempted with disobedience. If you find yourself on any one of these, stop! Turn around and set your face towards obedience and spiritual authority.

Step 1. Communication breakdown. You're silent. You've been hurt deeply by someone above you and you just don't want to talk.

Step 2. Ungratefulness. You begin to weigh the value of your church, family, work or government against its detriments.

Step 3. Stubbornness. You refuse to follow orders correctly. You're always editing, proving to yourself that your ideas are better.

Step 4. Open Rebellion. You want an equal voice with those in authority above you.

Step 5. The wrong friends. "Birds of a feather flock together." Your bad spirit will attract similar friends.

Step 6. Building a defense for wrongdoing. Self-authority produces in you a lower standard for your morals.

Step 7. Condemning others. You start spending your time looking for the hypocrites.

Step 8. Depression. Satan comes in with the clincher and accuses you. The danger is suicide: Mental, moral, spiritual, or even physical.

A MESSAGE FOR LEADERS

If leaders are not careful, they can cause an environment that fosters rebellion. I have seen this especially in churches. Even though this message applies to all areas of leadership I will address it to church leaders, and especially pastors.

Pastors, you can not motivate your church to righteousness by using witchcraft in the pulpit. I know this is a strong statement but let me explain to you three methods of control I have seen pastors use on their congregations, instead of allowing the Holy Ghost to govern.

Condemnation. We know that in Christ that there is no condemnation. But many pastors feel this is the method to use to communicate the gospel and its righteousness to their people. How far from the truth this is.

You need to understand that condemnation is different from godly conviction. I have been asked by many, "How can you tell the difference between the two?" It's simple. Godly conviction leaves when you tell God you are sorry. Condemnation doesn't. It hangs on you like Napalm, burning your spirit. And, if the fire is not quenched, it will blaze into full-blown rebellion.

Manipulation. You cannot trick people into righteousness. Many television ministries have come to the realization that people are tired of receiving letters asking for prayer when they are really pleas begging for money.   Pastors, we cannot create emergencies to finance hobbies, or invent scary predictions about the rapture to call them to the altar. The end does not justify the means.   We must be honest and straightforward, and let God worry about the results.

Intimidation. I saved this one for last because it is the biggest. I know literally hundreds of ministers who will not move into the full will of God because of peer pressure. This is multiplied many times over in local churches where pastors use the pulpit as a whip, knowing that if someone gets out of line all they need to do is call the name from the pulpit and that saint will be browbeaten into obedience. Many saints are fraught today with a heart of rebellion because some pastor used the wicked spirit of intimidation.

At my pastorate in San Francisco a young girl got into serious trouble. An older saint in the church came and asked me why I did not call this young woman's name out from the pulpit? I replied that the poor sister had already suffered rejection and humiliation from her family and she also must give birth to a fatherless baby. Do you think it makes me a man to stand in front of a thousand people and humiliate this helpless young woman? I don't think so, and I won't do it.

THE PERFECT EXAMPLE: JESUS

Jesus was just 12 years old when His parents took Him to the temple in Jerusalem. When His parent's business at the temple was done they unknowingly left Jesus behind. After a day's journey they realized that Jesus was not with them. Upon arriving back at the temple they found Jesus teaching and astonishing the leaders of the temple by His understanding of the word of God. Jesus proved that He, at twelve years old, was capable of beginning His ministry. Yet He waited eighteen long years before His ministry began. Luke wrote that, when He left with Mary and Joseph He was "subject to them."[53]

---

[53] Luke 2:51

If we could only learn that, when it is time for our ministry to flower, God will do it. Abraham had two sons. Ishmael was a son of the flesh (the ministry *man* got started) and Isaac was a son of promise (the ministry God got started). Just remember, Ishmael didn't die!

HOW TO DISOBEY
CHAPTER 4

There are times that you are going to have to disobey those in authority over you. The key to this is knowing when you, as a Christian, must disobey and when you must be obedient, lest you infect yourself with the spirit of rebellion. There is a fine line between the two and I will try to make this division as clear as possible.

WHY SHOULD A CHRISTIAN EVER DISOBEY?

There will be times when those in authority will ask you to do something that a Christian cannot take part in. During these situations it is important that you have a clear understanding of these two facts:

1. You are not alone. Many people in the word of God exemplified acts of disobedience according to their God-given convictions.

2. God will greatly reward you if it is done properly.

The danger of disobeying authority is obvious. It can put you into the position of rebelliousness. You must understand that God utterly hates a rebellious spirit. This is the reason satan was removed from heaven. God will not tolerate nor allow this kind of spirit to dwell in any of His people. That is why Samuel called rebellion "witchcraft"[54], because it is a spirit of satan. You must have a clear understanding of this because the only way you can disobey properly is to keep your spirit clear.

Yvonne, a sister in our church, came to me concerning her work in the purchasing department of a large bank in San Francisco. She worriedly questioned, "Richard, what should I do? An officer of the bank came and threw some purchase orders on my desk and told me to sign them. When I looked at

them, they were for large pieces of
equipment. I was asked to sign as if I had
seen this equipment and could verify that the
purchase had been made. When I saw this,
God convicted me and I felt like I could not
sign them. Tomorrow I am going to have to
go to work and I know this officer is going to
demand my signatures. If I don't give them
he'll probably fire me!"

"Do you feel that this officer is being
dishonest?" I asked.

"No, he seems to be an honest person. I
just felt that I couldn't sign for the purchases
of something I couldn't verify."

"Then you must obey what God is telling
you, but at the same time you must be sure
that your actions are not interpreted as an
accusation against this man, as though you're
doubting his honesty."

Yvonne went back to her work place and
the worst of all possibilities happened. She
humbly told this man she could not sign the
papers. He immediately blew up and
threatened to fire her on the spot, but instead

chose to write up a reprimand regarding her office skills. He then grabbed the documents and went to find someone else to sign them.

A few weeks later she was visited by a superior from her headquarters office. He came to see her concerning the criticism his office had received about her performance as a secretary. As they walked into a counseling room her heart skipped a beat as the officer said, "I know it is unprecedented for someone from the main office to make an inquiry of this type concerning one reprimand, but the report that was sent up by your superior was so severe and cutting that it was brought to my attention." He then asked her to take a seat and said, "Please be candid with me, what did you do that made him so mad?"

She simply told him the story she had shared with me.

"I thought so," he replied. "This man has been under investigation for nearly three months and is known to have been siphoning money from this corporation for years. We could not prove it and now we know why.

Nobody underneath him has stood up to his demand to falsify purchase orders. We are grateful to you, Yvonne, for being a woman of honesty and integrity." Yvonne said she would never forget his last words as he stood at the door: "Thanks for standing up."

A few days later the investigation was completed and the guilty parties were exposed. Most were fired, but Yvonne was promoted!

I like that investigator's statement, "Thanks for standing up." It brings to one's mind Shadrach, Meshach and Abednego. These three Hebrew children were brought as slaves to Babylon. They became promoted to oversee the affairs of King Nebuchadnezzar's province after Daniel interpreted his dream. The king later built a large idol to be worshipped and told everyone in the kingdom that when they heard the sound of music they were to bow to the golden idol.

The three Hebrews knew they were going to have to stand up and disobey this order, but notice how they did it. They did not get arrogant and defiant; they simply stood. When brought before the king they did not defend their actions but told the king it was against their convictions to bow before the idol but that they were willing to submit to the punishment of the king. They didn't threaten the king and say, "If you hurt us God will do something to you."

You can tell the king was impressed by their attitude, for he said, "I will give you another chance. This time just bow and we will forget the whole thing." But the Israelites knew that the second chance was useless, for this was a God-given conviction. What they were doing was disobeying in action, but obeying in attitude. So the king threw them into the fiery furnace.

Notice what happened when they landed in the furnace. The ropes that were binding them were burnt off and God came down and visited them and walked with them through the blaze. You see, their obedience in spirit attracted God Himself. This is the method of true godly disobedience. Don't let the spirit

"He says it tastes like humble pie?"

and anger of the world infect your spirit. Keep a good attitude and simply do not do what they are telling you to do.

Daniel faced a similar situation. He was told he couldn't pray but he knew he had to seek God. He disobeyed in action and prayed anyway. When brought before the king he willingly submitted to the punishment of being thrown into the lions' den. No wonder God shut the lions' mouths and delivered him; his spirit was pure!

I have seen many Christians stand up for something that is right but develop a wrong attitude, and they can't figure out why God punishes them. I met a woman recently who was asked to falsify some medical documents. She, also, decided to stand up for what was right but she took the issue to the union and created a scene at the hospital she worked for. Yes, the people who were wrong got punished, but so did this woman. She lost her job.

She told me that God stands up for those who are right and so why didn't He stand up for her? Her disobedience to the order of signing the documents was correct but in the process she developed an attitude of vengeance and God could not support her.

Peter and the apostles were told by the leaders of the temple not to preach in the name of Jesus. To this they had to disobey. Notice their obedience in spirit. When they were whipped and beaten they rejoiced because they were counted worthy to suffer for the name of Jesus. Wow! What an attitude.

Each of us needs to develop the humility of spirit that is found in some of the underground churches in communist Russia. Terry Law, author of many popular books, told me it was not unusual to see the Russian flag displayed in many of these underground meetings. Look at the contrast.

Here are people defying their government's orders against religious assemblies and yet at the same time displaying their country's flag, thereby showing loyalty to their nation. Their act of disobedience by worshiping did not affect their spirit of obedience to the rest of their nation's laws which did <u>not</u> violate God's laws. No wonder God is currently bringing godless communism to its knees.

Compare this to some of the scenes that are being acted out in front of abortion clinics across America. Have Christians begun to take on the tactics of the world? Do we model ourselves after Mahatma Gandhi and Martin Luther King or after the man Christ Jesus?

A friend of mine who spent three months protesting in front of abortion clinics in the San Francisco Bay Area said he finally had to quit because of the mood of the demonstrations he took part in: The spirit of "rebellion" was present. Paul said, "Do not be overcome by evil but overcome evil with good."[55]

I do believe abortion is a horrible evil, but I disagree with the notion that we should

---

[54] 1 Samuel 15:23
[55] Romans 12:21

fight evil using carnal methods. Paul again said," ...the weapons of our warfare are not carnal but mighty in God for pulling down strongholds."[56]   We must stand up against evil but HOW do we do so?

I will deal with this subject more thoroughly in the chapter entitled, "Spiritual Warfare." Let me make this clear: I do not stand for passive Christianity. Christianity must be assertive, powerful and done through God!

DON'T BE DECEPTIVE

When you are asked by someone in authority to do something that is against your conscience, you should not cover your disobedience by deception. Remember, Daniel opened up his window and prayed just as he always had done. He did not hide in a closet where no one could see him. He could easily have made everyone in the kingdom think he was obeying the king's edict by not praying openly and then sneak around when

---

[56] 2 Corinthians 10:4

no one was looking and pray anyway. But this would have been deceitful.

A man working at a used car lot was asked by his boss to lie about a car that was for sale. He was instructed to tell prospective buyers that the car had only been owned by one family and most of the miles were freeway miles. The truth was, it had been driven by a teenage drug dealer and the car had been obtained through a police auction. He mentioned to me that he couldn't tell these prospective buyers a lie, and so would tell them the truth.

I asked him if he had shared this decision with his boss. He told me he did not feel that it was important to let him know, that what his boss didn't know wouldn't hurt him. I told him he could not be deceptive by covering up the fact that he was not going to tell the lie of his boss. This would be just as wrong.

You can't make someone believe a lie, to tell the truth. This man heeded my counsel and the next day informed his boss that his conscience had bothered him and that he could no longer be deceptive about the cars he was selling. The response of his boss floored him. He told him to pack up his things, clean out his desk, and leave within the hour!

Within ten minutes he had loaded most of his personal belongings into his car. Standing there on the side of the road, looking at his former place of employment, he questioned God. "Is this my reward for standing up for what is right?"

Before the words were out of his mouth he was approached by a man who managed the new Honda dealership down the street. The dealer told him he had been watching his work for the past few months and wondered if my friend would be willing to come and work for him. The only catch was, he needed him to start immediately because of an emergency that had happened to one of their salesmen.

My friend just laughed. God had known about this position all along and had realized that the only way He could get him to the

Honda dealership immediately was to get him fired from the used car lot!

You will never experience great deliverances unless you are placed in positions of tension. Don't dodge the conflicts of persecution, because in these experiences lie the makings of great miracles.

HONESTY~A LONELY WORD
CHAPTER 5

I was quite excited when a close friend of mine (whom I will call George) phoned to tell me he was quitting his job at a large firm and was going full-time into the ministry and would be working on the staff of a large church. This excited me because for years I had been encouraging George to do this very thing. I have often seen some of the most talented Christians give their abilities to a secular enterprise rather than using their talents for God.

After George had been working at this church for a week he was offered a position with his former company that would pay him an annual salary in the six-figure bracket.

George told me how good it felt to reject the position, even though this was the dream of a lifetime and he would have been given the title of chief executive officer of this company.

As his tenure at the church continued he began to notice things were not as they had previously seemed to have been. He observed that something was wrong when the men on the staff were not encouraged to give honest reports about their ministries.

The next revelation shocked him. He discovered that the church had been trading favors with politicians. He knew that if the newspapers ever discovered this the reputation of the church would be blown sky-high. We spent long hours into the night talking about Christian ethics in the church.

He finally decided that he would need to go back to secular employment for the sake of his conscience . When I heard this news I literally broke into tears because a young man had found more integrity and ethical management in the world than he had in the church!

Billy Joel is a secular "pop" songwriter who has, as far as I know, had no experience with Jesus. But the words to one of his songs scream out to me. Here's a man of the world crying out for something that the church should be clamoring for:

"Honesty is such a lonely word.

Everyone is so untrue;

honesty is such a lonely word

it's hardly ever heard;

but it's all I want from you."

Before I began pastoring a church, I'd toured with our singing group called "Richard and the Redeemed." I had written numerous songs, and experienced marginal success in gospel music circles. One day while I was in Texas at a large Christian celebration, I was pleasantly surprised to hear a group singing one of my songs, "No Grave." They had announced the wrong title but that was OK, for they said the song was recorded on their latest album which would be on sale in the lobby. I was excited!

This was one of the first times a fairly well-known group had recorded one of my songs. I was quickly in line to buy a disc. When I received it I flipped it over to see my song in print and there underneath the title was the statement "author unknown."

Boy was I upset! I couldn't wait until the singers got off the stage so I could let them know who the unknown author was. Standing at the back of the auditorium, fuming, waiting for their concert to end, the Lord spoke to me in a flash that will take me a paragraph to explain. He said:

"What are you so upset about? You've stood before congregations and told people I gave you those songs. Now, as soon as you don't get credit, you're all upset. Whose songs are they, yours or Mine? Did not I tell you, 'Freely you have received so freely give?'"

By the time the Lord was through with me I was on my knees. I had suddenly realized that with my music I had been mainly concerned about getting credit and gaining wealth from God's gift. I felt like a money changer in the temple. When I got back to San Francisco I met with a lawyer and lifted all the copyrights from my music.

I had to be honest. How could I charge someone else for singing a song the Lord gave me? Isn't that the spirit of the world? Everyone is so concerned about getting the glory and renumeration for their God-given gifts. What if the Bible was copyrighted and we had to pay fees to the Catholic church for its use? Does your pastor copyright his sermons?

A new day is dawning in the church. A day when musicians will be purified to the point of reaching their true position in the kingdom of God. Satan had the highest rank that God could give any angel. He was in charge of God's choir and music. Ezekiel wrote that music was literally created in satan's body. But satan wanted to get credit and be exalted. No wonder satan still uses music today to influence his servants. How much more effort should we exert to restore music to its rightful place.

I recently read a popular Christian music magazine, and a Christian singer was complaining about the trials of being a star and having everyone watching his every move. He complained that he needed more understanding from his fans. What a joke! Jesus is the only "star" the church needs. Any other idol that is set up needs to come down so that Jesus alone is glorified.

I believe the day is coming when Christian musicians will be afraid to charge exorbitant fees for their concerts, or ask for royalty payments from worshippers who use their lyrics to commune with God.

Honesty is the act of being vulnerable and being willing to admit that you, no matter how great your position might be, are still susceptible to failure. I once was preaching at a church out in the Northwest countryside. After I'd finished my sermon the rugged pastor came towards the pulpit to give an invitation to the altar. He suddenly slumped over the pulpit and burst into tears, sobbing these words into the microphone :

"People, I have a confession to make. I have been a phony. A young girl moved into our town from Los Angeles and she was pregnant with an illegitimate baby. I told her that we didn't want her kind in our church and asked her to take the next plane back to where she came from. She's here tonight, and I know this might embarrass her, but I need her help. I beg her to forgive me and, if she will, come forward to pray for this old pastor that he might find peace with God."

The beautiful young girl, who was obviously pregnant, slipped out of her seat and quietly came down the aisle with her head bowed. You could tell she was nervous. Some thoughtful women quickly slipped out of their seats and joined her as she gently laid her hand on the head of the pastor who was weeping in a kneeling position on the platform. She then began to speak in tongues as she was filled with the Holy Ghost for the first time!

The scene at the altar was soon interrupted by a large lumberjack-type man who leaped from his seat and barreled down to the altar for his own session of repentance. After this man had wept for a while he came to me for counsel. He told me he had been part of a conspiracy with some other board members to split this church. They had already hired a young man from Bible school to become their pastor, and at that moment he was on a bus heading toward the church.

The man explained to me that he had never seen the pastor be this honest before. He had only known him as an infallible leader. When the pastor was honest and confessed his mistake, it revealed to the board member his own sinful heart. I soon got this man and the others together for a full reconciliation. The young Bible school student got a free bus ticket home...where he belonged!

Darkness has no energy within itself because it is just the absence of light. Sin in a man's heart has the same attributes as darkness. If you wish to remove darkness from the room you don't try to vacuum it out. Instead, you simply turn on the light. It is

"For the third time, Peter, do you know Jesus of Nazareth?"

the same phenomena that happens in the heart.

When one person is honest it causes all those around to suddenly see the need for purity within their own hearts.

For years I was bothered with the problem of lust. There were many times I was afraid I was going to be exposed or maybe even yield to sin. In the past I had gone to some ministers and hinted about my problem. When they caught the drift they patted me on the shoulder and said:

"Son, every man has that problem. Just believe the grace of God will get you through."

But I knew this was wrong. I knew one day I would probably pastor a church and that I must conquer this wickedness now, lest the fear of losing my reputation cause me to cover it up. One day I was riding in a car with a district superintendent of my denomination. I asked him about this problem. Of course I told him I was asking about it for a friend's sake. I inquired,

"What would you do if a young man had a problem with lust and he was afraid that it might lead him to committing a sin"?

"Well," he said in his comfortable drawl, "I'd have to take him in before the board, 'cause it's my responsibility as a leader in this district to expose all sin."

I responded quickly, "You know, I think my friend has just gotten over this problem anyway. Don't bother."

I left this meeting with a sinking feeling within my heart. I realized that there was not an environment within my organization that allowed people to be honest. The last place I now wanted to go was to church leadership, because they were more concerned about looking like righteous judges than in restoration.

A year had passed and I was staying at a hotel on a business trip when this problem again reared up its ugly head. That night it was revealed to me that it was a problem that only the power of God could eradicate from my life and I needed help from someone strong in the Holy Ghost.

There was a convention going on nearby, sponsored by another Pentecostal denomination, so I decided to go there to see if I could get some help. After service I saw a group of ministers and asked them if they would pray with me and see if God would reveal to them the root of my problem. The men began to pray quietly. After about 20 minutes of prayer one of them said:

"The phrase 'Sixteen years old' keeps coming to me. Does this mean anything to you?"

When he said those words, an event that I had completely erased from my memory suddenly flashed before me. I knew this was the source of my problem. The men instructed me that if I didn't want to share what God was revealing, I didn't need to. But I assured them that this problem had been with me too long and that I needed complete deliverance.

The event that God reminded me of happened when I was staying over at the house of a friend. He had attacked me while I was sleeping and I awoke to discover he was a homosexual. I was so upset I ran out of the house and walked in my T-shirt through the cold and foggy streets of San Francisco until I reached my home. I slipped into my bed and never told my parents nor anyone else what had transpired that night.

Since then, satan had plagued my subconscious mind with the need to lust after women to prove I had no part in that event. Well, at that moment I knew I had received complete deliverance! Now that it is years later, I have been able to share this experience with my congregation and have seen hundreds receive their own deliverance from hidden sins that had given satan a door of opportunity through which to pass and oppress their walk with God.

You can be free from concealed sins that are oppressing you, but it is going to take honesty on your part and the part of leadership. When you are sharing your faults and failures with people, you are going to feel like the loneliest person in the world. But honesty is the road to true freedom.

One Sunday morning I stepped to the church pulpit, and suddenly realized I definitely didn't have a message from God because I hadn't prayed earlier. I could have probably thrown something together and faked it through the morning sermon, but instantly God said, "Why don't you just be honest!" So I was.

I turned to the church and told them I didn't have anything from God, so I wasn't going to preach! I asked the other ministers behind me if they had something, but they said they didn't, so I turned back to the congregation and promised them that if they'd come back to the Sunday night service they would hear a message from God. That night they did.

What is it that makes us want to lie? Pride? Fear? Self-preservation? Probably all of these. The prophet Ezekiel gives us an insight into why religious people lie:

"Son of man, these men have set up their idols in their hearts...Everyone...who sets up idols in his heart...and then comes to the prophet, I the LORD will answer him who comes, according to the multitude of his idols."[57]

Satan is called the "father of liars." If you will look at the way Ezekiel describes these idols of the heart, it's like he's describing the spirit of lies. God says He will answer us according to these lying spirits. This is why many religious people can be caught in such blatant hypocrisy.

Jesus told us if satan finds a house swept clean he will go and get seven more spirits worse than himself to possess this "swept" person, which explains why one lie always leads into a greater lie. Another point that this verse from Ezekiel makes is that God will allow you to think that a lie you believe is from Him, even though it is not. It's kind of a heavenly deception. No wonder the Pharisees were so sure that they were on God's side when they crucified Jesus.

---

[57] Ezekial 14:3,4

To some of you this may sound scary, but you don't have to worry as long as you "keep a broken and contrite spirit" before the Lord. We are not to stand in our own righteousness but in the righteousness of Jesus Christ. Whenever you start defending yourself, look out! Danger signs should pop up all over your mind.

To your own self you must be true. One time I was at a holiness conference in Anaheim, California. A pastor friend of mine and I were staying at a hotel near the conference. My friend was abruptly called back home to his church for an emergency and I realized that I would have to spend the night alone. Suddenly satan put the thought in my mind to view a film that was on the hotel video network. It wasn't necessarily an evil film, but it was something that this Christian shouldn't see.

I sat in the morning service listening to Leonard Ravenhill preach on holiness and at the same time I fought with the turmoil in my mind, whether I was or wasn't going to watch this film. I finally decided I needed help so I called up my best friend, my wife, and asked her if she would come to Anaheim. She happily flew to my side and that night the film was no longer an issue.

My wife and I have a vulnerable relationship with each other. We are unafraid to be honest about our faults. It is this kind of honesty that is going to establish your walk with Jesus in a sure place.

You need to be careful about sharing things with your mate or close friends that could cause them to stumble, if they are not strong enough to bear it. I have seen many Christian marriages suffer when the partners unnecessarily unloaded their past sins. I counseled with a married couple that experienced extreme marital difficulties when the wife confessed that she had gone through an abortion before they got married. The husband still has a hard time forgiving her. Some things are too sensitive to share with those you love. If they do need to be shared, confide in a minister.

I don't know everything about Sandy's past and she doesn't know everything about mine. If Jesus forgives and forgets, we need to learn to do the same. The only time you need to confess a sin of the past is when its oppression is out of your control. Even then, you need to be extremely cautious about whom you confess it to.

REALITY OR HYPOCRISY

In a Christian's search for a deeper walk with God, he's going to be faced with reality or hypocrisy. It is impossible for you to just do the righteous thing, without truly believing it in your heart. If you don't believe, it will turn to hypocrisy. Let me explain.

There were two men who lived in our Men's Home and one evening they got into a heated argument. As the dispute progressed, the whole house was awakened by the racket. One of the men, when he saw what he had done to the others in the house, immediately repented and said he was sorry. The other man also said he was sorry but he only said it with his lips. He was not sorry in his heart.

This is hypocrisy when you do the right thing only because it is expected of you, and not because you desire to be like Jesus. Three days later the unforgiving man called me in desperation. He had purchased a gun and was ready to shoot the other man. For three days he had been obsessed with vengeance, though he had previously voiced forgiveness. He had not yet really forgiven the other man. This smoldering spiritual hypocrisy had ignited a blazing fire of hate!

The search for spiritual authority cannot be taken on by a novice. Jesus is not a club that you join, nor a bumper sticker that you adhere to your BMW. Christianity is a life that must be lived with consistency~ everywhere. Isaiah talks about a people that transgressed against God and were full of sin:

"They seek Me daily, and delight to know My ways as a nation that did righteousness."[58]

Isaiah is referring to "groupie" Christians. One day when I was visiting a

---

[58] Isaiah 58:2

"mega" church, I went to the front along with the others who were going to pray the sinner's prayer. As I was standing in line I couldn't help but hear the comment of one of the girls that was in front of me.

"Isn't this really groovy? All of my friends are doing this 'saved' thing. I'm so excited."

At the conference I mentioned earlier in this chapter, Leonard Ravenhill made this comment:

"The abortions that are upsetting God are not happening in the abortion clinics of America, but are happening at the altars of our churches. People need to come to God and repent."

David said, "You desire truth in the *inward* parts."[59]

---

[59] Psalm 51:6

MONEY MATTERS
CHAPTER 6

Solomon relates a parable in the book of Ecclesiastes that makes an interesting point I feel is pertinent to Christians who revel in poverty. I'll paraphrase the story.

There once was a small quaint town that had hardy men living in it. Though the town was not large the people were happy and lived peaceable lives with those around. One day a dark gloomy cloud of depression fell upon the hearts of the men of the city, for a powerful, mighty king declared war against them. The king roared onto the countryside with huge machines of war. He even built traps outside the city wall to catch unsuspecting citizens that might wander off. The men of this village were in a quandary over what to do. Finally, they decided that surrender was going to be their only option.

In this town there also lived a poor godly man with barely enough money to feed his family. He was always in debt and never paid his bills on time. His family wore the most meager clothes, but he was a good godly man. He decided to pray and ask God for an answer to the city's plight and sure enough, true to His word ("If any of you lacks wisdom, let him ask of God, who gives to all liberally"),[60] God gave him the most clever method of defeating the attacking king. By the next day his plan was implemented, the king's army was destroyed and the town was peaceful again.

A few months later the poor godly man decided to start a church, thinking that everyone would remember him because of the great wisdom he had imparted which had saved the city. But guess what? They didn't remember.

Solomon contemplated this when he said:

---

[60] James 1:5

"Wisdom is better than strength. Nevertheless the poor man's wisdom is despised."[61]

I have experienced poverty; Sandy and I were once not able to buy food for a meal. I have also experienced wealth; I made $120,000.00 in 1987. Wealth is better, and you are definitely taken more seriously when you show success in your personal life. Many times the world looks at Christians and sees our lives so out of kilter and filled with unfulfilled promises, such as debts, that we aren't taken seriously.

I am not talking about extravagant luxuriance, but rather controlled wealth. If we are to possess this earth and take dominion over it, then we had better "get it together" in our ability to manage money. This is why it is so absurd for those with prosperous ministries, and pastors who have had great financial success, to squander their money on unnecessary expensive clothes, cars and homes. The year that I made that large sum of money I also drove a Yugo (the

---

[61] Ecclesiastes 9:16

"Have you been playing around Job's hedge again?"

most inexpensive car sold in America at the time) as my personal car. I did this not to feign humility, but because it made economical sense.

I am the first to admit that I am a poor manager of money. When Sandy and I first got married a visiting minister told me that if I was the man of the house I should manage the money. I said, "O.K." So I told Sandy, "From now on, I am going to pay the bills and handle all the family finances." Within three months our checkbook was so messed up that we had to close the account. Checks had been bouncing higher then my wife's tolerance level.

She finally had mercy on me and closed the checking account, found all of the unpaid bills, and put us back on a workable family budget. After about six months of measured spending we were living in the black again. Even today, though, this blot on our credit record is brought up whenever we fill out loan papers for a large purchase.

You do not have to be an expert at fiscal policies to be in a good financial situation. I am a prime example of that. Even though I cannot personally manage money, our family finances and budget are in control and we are in a very secure position. By world standards we might even be considered wealthy. For example, I am writing this book in a Swiss villa in the Bavarian Alps. From the window I can view some of the most exotic skiing slopes in the world.

The church I pastor in San Francisco is financially secure. We own an entire city block. Our building is over 100,000 square feet and the sanctuary can accommodate 2,000 people on comfortable theater seats. Everything is paid in full, from our Heidelburg printing press to the building itself! If you'll admit your weakness and enlist God's help, He will make your deficiency a strength.

Our church finances are managed by my mother, Rev. Marilynn Gazowsky, who is a financial genius and has written a book on the subject entitled "Awake The Dawn." The problem is, most Christians who are poor managers of money have their ego in the way. Therefore they say, "It is God's will for me to be broke all the time," or when they do get money, they spend it so foolishly that they end up backsliding. In response to this train of thought someone once asked me, "Wasn't Jesus poor?"

WAS JESUS POOR?

Most people have a preconceived idea that Jesus lived in poverty all of His life. If you study the Scriptures I'm sure you will gain quite a different perspective of our Master's lifestyle. I will say at the outset, He definitely did not flaunt His wealth. But we also do not find Him begging for money either.

When I ask people if Jesus was poor the first statement they make is:

"Of course He was. Didn't Jesus say, 'Foxes have holes and birds of the air have nests, but the Son of man has nowhere to lay His head'"?[62]

---

[62] Luke 9:58

But wait a minute. Let's put that Scripture in its proper setting and see what Jesus was really saying. Seven verses before, Jesus was traveling through Samaria on His way to Jerusalem. If you remember the Lord's conversation with the woman at the well, the Samaritans did not worship God in Jerusalem. They believed that God should be worshiped in their mountains.

So, when Jesus came to Samaria to spend the night it greatly offended the Samaritans that Jesus was not going to worship with them, but instead was on His way to Jerusalem to worship with the Jews. When the Lord asked His disciples to have them prepare a place for Him to stay in the town the Samaritans kicked them out.

This made James and John upset and they said, "...Lord, do You want us to command fire to come down from Heaven and consume them, just as Elijah did?"[63]

Jesus quickly rebuked His disciples for their bad attitudes and they moved on to another village. A man soon joined himself

---

[63] Luke 9:54

• 118 •

with Jesus' party and asked the Lord, "Can I follow you?" Jesus responded to his question and explained the cost of discipleship when He told him,"...the Son of man has nowhere to lay His head."[64]

As you can see from the accompanying circumstances, Jesus had no place to stay that particular night. There is a Scripture that infers Jesus did indeed have a house. In John's gospel is this account:

"Then Jesus turned, and seeing them following, said to them, 'What do you seek?' They said to Him, 'Rabbi' (which is to say, when translated, Teacher), **Where are You staying?'** He said to them, 'Come and see.' They came and saw where He was staying, and remained with Him that day (now it was about the tenth hour)."[65]

Those disciples evidently spent the night at Jesus' house.

How many of you reading this book have a personal treasurer? Jesus did. The job was delegated to Judas and he must have had to

---

[64] Ibid. 9:58
[65] John 1:38-39

deal with some fairly serious sums of money because Jesus often traveled with an entourage. What if a man flew from New York to Los Angeles and spent over $250,000 on that trip? Would you say that was an extravagant amount of money? What if this man was the President of the United States?

Any time he travels he must take along a retinue of security agents, fly in a specially-designed airplane, and have a general alongside him carrying the black box that gives him instant access to all of our military stations around the world in case of a threat to national security. Suddenly this trip begins to look like a bargain.

So it was with Jesus. Whenever He traveled He had to support and feed his apostles and closest friends.[66]

He also had a group of financial supporters. Some of them were obviously wealthy because they were associated with well-known figures:

---

[66] Luke 8:1

"Joanna the wife of Chuza, Herod's steward, and Susanna, and many others who provided for Him from their substance."[67]

But what about his clothes? Didn't He dress like a beggar? No, He didn't. As a matter of fact, Jesus wore designer clothes. They were so impressive that John the Apostle describes a scene where the Roman soldiers conducted a mini-lottery to see who would win His garments:

"Then the soldiers, when they had crucified Jesus, took His garments and made four parts, to each soldier a part, and also the tunic. Now the tunic was without seam, woven from the top in one piece. They said therefore among themselves, "Let us not tear it, but cast lots for it, whose it shall be."[68]

How many of you brothers have a seamless suit? I am sure that Jesus did not wear it to show off the latest fashion but instead it served a practical purpose and most likely as a spiritual type (that I will not mention here).

---

[67] Luke 8:3
[68] John 19:23,24

But the Bible says, "He became poor."[69] What about that Scripture?

Wait a minute! Don't stop there; read the rest of the verse. "...that you through His poverty might become rich!"[70]

Jesus purposely died in poverty, leaving everything behind, so we might live in spiritual and physical wealth, and that more abundantly. Don't you see? The media, satan and the spirit of this world would love to keep Christians in poverty, and especially away from any positions of power and influence. That is why there has been such a mass media blitz against Christians having wealth.

We must resist this mindset because we know that satan is the god of this world (system), and he is not going to let go of control easily. Don't forget that Jesus told us, "The laborer is worthy of his wages."[71] And,the prophet Haggai said, "The silver is

---

69 2 Corinthians 8:9
70 Ibid. 8:9
71 Luke 10:7

Mine and the gold is Mine, says the LORD of hosts."[72]

FINANCIAL SUCCESS

Let's "get it together" in the area of our finances. On your road to spiritual authority, people are not going to listen to you if you are not successful in this simple area. If you're walking around broke all the time constantly going to family members for loans, and straining your relationships because you can't pay for your own meal when you go to a restaurant, you surely will not have much influence in the spiritual realm.

Jesus said, "If you have not been faithful in the unrighteous mammon (money), who will commit to your trust the true riches? And if you have not been faithful in what is another man's, who will give you what is your own?"[73]

My grandpa often said, "Poor folk have poor ways." Have you ever thought, "How

---

[72] Haggai 2:8
[73] Luke 16:11-12

can poor people help poor people?" If you're always in need of money, you surely won't be able to play the part of the good Samaritan,who helped the man who had been assaulted by thieves.

This good Samaritan obviously was not broke, for he had enough money to leave some with the innkeeper for the injured man's full recovery. How many of us have enough extra money to pay someone's hospital bill for any length of time?

It seems funny to address the subject of tithing in a book that is dealing with a deeper walk with God. Most of you reading this book should have already figured this one out and are faithful tithers to your local church. But if you haven't, this one's for you.

Tithing predated the Old Testament law so it is not technically required by it. Abraham paid tithes before the Old Testament was written by Moses, his "grandson", many generations later. I'm sure Abraham had a clear understanding that everything he owned was the Lord's in the first place, and by giving God the first 10% of his income, he was insuring God's blessing upon the remaining 90%.

If you want God to bless your finances, don't think you can hold back on your tithes. Tithing is a spiritual principle that transcends the law and was mentioned by Jesus in a positive light when He said: "You **tithe mint and rue and all manner of herbs,** and pass by justice and the love of God. These you ought to have done, **without leaving the others undone."** [74] A tithe should be the first thing taken care of after receiving your paycheck, for it is the "firstfruit". Solomon put it this way:

"Honor the LORD with your possessions, and with the firstfruits of all your increase; so your barns will be filled with plenty, and your vats will overflow with new wine." [74]

The prophet Malachi said it more strongly. "Will a man rob God? Yet you have robbed Me! But you say, 'In what way have we robbed You?' In tithes and

[74] Luke 11:42
[75] Proverbs 3:9-10

• 125 •

offerings. You are cursed with a curse. For you have robbed Me, even this whole nation. Bring all the tithes into the storehouse, that there may be food in My house, and prove Me now in this," says the LORD of hosts, "If I will not open for you the windows of heaven and pour out for you such blessing that there will not be room enough to receive it."[76]

You should pay your tithes to the church you regularly attend and not to some evangelist or other ministry. As you can see in the previous Scripture, the prophet was speaking about the house of the Lord where you worship. If you're not a member of a local church, I'm surprised you made it this far through the book!

[76] Malachi 3:8-10

THE ART OF WAR
CHAPTER 7

Each of us has a desire for spiritual authority, and for the ability to conduct war against satan effectively. Paul told us:

"...Being ready to punish all disobedience when your obedience is fulfilled."[77]

You will not be able to skillfully conduct warfare against satan if you are walking in disobedience to authority. He will know it, and will be totally unafraid of you. Take the time to make past mistakes right.

If you have rebelled against leadership, go back and correct the mistakes and bind up all hurts you may have left behind in your rush to the top. If you don't heal those

---

[77] 2 Corinthians 10:6

relationships, you will make yourself very vulnerable to an attack by satan. All he'll need to do is bring up the past at an opportune time to ruin the effectiveness of your ministry.

I recently counseled a pastor who had committed adultery early in his ministry but was never properly restored. The problem was just "swept under the carpet" and his wife hadn't even been consulted. Three years later his ministry was in full swing when suddenly someone, who knew the situation was not dealt with properly, thought it was their duty to reveal it to his wife.

Instantly the problem was as ugly as if it had happened the previous day. He lost his effectiveness in the church and went through enormous struggles in his marriage. He finally moved to another city to start over again. Satan's counterattack on his ministry was very effective and almost totally paralyzed it. But the problem ended up still not being corrected. When people in leadership fall into sin, Paul told Timothy,

"Those who are sinning rebuke in the presence of all ,that the rest also may fear."[78]

This may be an embarrassing procedure, but it clears the minister in two areas. It allows for full confession and restoration, and it also protects him from anyone disclosing his past later. Since this brother had not been Biblically reprimanded, his ministry unto the Lord was again assailable.

Sure enough, two years later the woman whom he had originally committed adultery with decided that his punishment was not severe enough. This woman went to his district superintendent and suddenly he was dealing with the whole problem again. By this time he was pastoring another church and eventually lost it, too!

Do not leave yourself susceptible to satanic attacks like this. You may not think it's war, but I can guarantee you, satan does. The moment you become a Christian, satan levels the sights of his fiery darts at your mind and waits for an opportunity to strike. Don't wait for him to get you. The best way

---

[78] 1 Timothy 5:20

to engage in warfare with this kind of an enemy is to fight *offensively*. This war is not fought on our territory, but at the "gates of hell."[79]

RULES OF WAR

In an ancient book written by the Chinese General, Sun Tzu, in 600 B.C. called the Art of War, we find a most interesting guide to military warfare. This book has influenced generals throughout history and today is still required reading in military academies around the world. Sun Tzu writes:

"Some people are intelligent in knowing themselves but stupid in knowing their opponents, and for others the reverse is true. Neither kind can solve the problem of learning and applying the laws of war."[80]

Your best defense is knowing yourself and your weaknesses, for you will never conduct effective war until you do. You can strengthen your spiritual defenses by doing some of the following which I have mentioned in previous chapters:

[79] Matthew 16:18

1. Put yourself under proper authority.

2. Make sure your past sins have been dealt with correctly.

3. Be honest about your own weaknesses and seek help to straighten out these areas.

4. Get your finances under control.

If you know yourself you will have an effective protection against satan. As Sun Tzu stated: Know your opponent. This concurs with what Paul the Apostle said, "...lest satan should take advantage of us; for we are not ignorant of his devices".[81]

SATAN THE TERRORIST

Whenever an opponent in war is stronger than you, the rules of war say you should never directly engage them. This is why satan does not directly attack you, because he knows that the Holy Ghost in you is greater than himself. Satan is forced to avoid direct confrontation so he uses terrorist tactics.

---

[81] 2 Corinthians 2:11

A terrorist always looks for the most vulnerable area of a nation to attack. Terrorists never attack strong military installations but instead look for areas of extreme susceptibility. Their purpose is not to destroy the enemy but to destabilize them and make them angry. If he can make you angry you are bound to make a mistake.

Take the example of Moaammar Khadhafi of Libya. He knows that if he directly defied the United States he would lose the battle within a matter of hours. So he has chosen, as satan also has against the church, to use terrorist tactics. He sent a few men to kill a crippled man in a wheelchair on a pleasure boat going across the Mediterranean Sea; he set off an explosion in an airport in Rome, killing American women and children; and a few months later he bombed some American soldiers partying in a West German disco. Each one of these attacks were designed to get the ultimate amount of news coverage, thereby increasing the destabilizing effect that the terrorists are after.

As Americans sit at home watching these events take place on their television screens,anger wells within them. This anger upsets their meals. You can listen to the radio talk shows and hear people mouthing off about their hate for terrorism. This is the desired effect. The American politicians respond by turning our airports into military battle zones so every American traveler is treated like a potential enemy. Once again, this is the desired outcome.

This is exactly how satan brings upheaval in a local church. He finds the most vulnerable member, such as a teenager who is experiencing problems already,and terrorizes this person and causes him to sin in a way that receives the most publicity. Let me give you an example. A teenage son of a church board member gets drunk and wrecks his father's car. The pastor is afraid that all the teenagers are going to run out and get drunk, so he rakes the whole congregation over the coals to make sure nobody will ever do this again. But in the process he disrupts the church. Remember, you'll never turn on the light by cursing the darkness.

Sometimes the situation even gets worse because "older" saints pick up on the pastor's message and begin giving every teenager in the church that "questioning look." Then satan receives an ally in their condemnation. The young people in the church feel they are all under attack and begin to find fault with their attackers, the very people they need the most. As you can see, just a few terrorist attacks of this type can disorganize an entire church and cause problems that will linger on for months and even years.

How does one deal with these terrorist attacks? I believe former President Reagan gave us a great example in his dealing with Khadhafi's terrorist acts. Your first response toward the *victims* of terrorism should be love and care, not alienation. Secondly, don't spend your time hunting the world for these peon terrorist soldiers. What Reagan did was identify the *source* of these terrorist attacks. Through much research these events were traced back to Libya.

A few weeks after the last terrorist act, our American military assault planes flew from their bases in Southern England and attacked the city of Tripoli and the headquarters of Khadhafi. This raid was so well planned and executed that the United States dropped a bomb right on Khadhafi's own bedroom! The results were dramatic. Suddenly Khadhafi had nothing more to say and the terrorist acts from his corner of the world immediately stopped.

An effective military campaign against the powers of satan must be conducted in a similar manner. Jesus told us, "No one can enter a strong man's house and plunder his goods, unless he first binds the strong man and then he will plunder his house."[82] A church must first take care of the war against the "strong man"(ruler of darkness). By doing this they'll stop terrorism. This also works in a family, business or otherwise.

Satan is afraid of direct confrontation and he trembles at the name of Jesus. Remember, we are stronger than him. Jesus told us, "When a strong man, fully armed, guards his own palace, his goods are in

---

[82] Mark 3:27

peace. But **when a stronger than he comes upon him and overcomes him,** he takes from him all his armor in which he trusted, and divides his spoils."[83]

As you can see, there are additional great blessings in warfare because you are then given a right to spoil satan's house!

PLUNDERING HIS HOUSE

The kingdoms of God and satan are territorial. The battle to be fought is a territorial one. God told Abraham, Moses, and Joshua that every place the soles of their feet would trod would be theirs. This is why Jesus could not die for our sins in Heaven. He had to come down to this earth and place His feet on the ground and "take the territory." When He did, satan's kingdom trembled.

When Jesus walked into a town or village He wasn't just sightseeing. He was taking territory and teaching His disciples to do the same. This is why the great commission is "to go." This means change your venue, or

---

[83] Luke 11: 21-22

move. You cannot fulfill this commission by standing still.

The Bible shows us that there are powers and principalities that rule over the earth. No wonder John said, "The whole world lies under the sway of the wicked one".[84]

Satan is highly organized and has a very structured kingdom. The Bible calls these "strongholds," which can be defined as patterns of thoughts that run through society. I have listed five major citadels that need to be destroyed by prayer warfare.

1. **National.** This stronghold runs parallel to the political government of a nation. If you have ever traveled from one country to another, you will find a different thinking pattern and a resistance to the gospel that is unique to each. Daniel warred against the prince of Persia, which was a sophisticated monarchy of wicked spirits who were arrayed to hinder the message from coming to Daniel.

---

[84] 1 John 5:19

As Daniel fasted and prayed for twenty-one days, a battle went on in the heavenly realm. It was so intense that Michael himself had to come down to fight against the prince of Persia. He finally prevailed and the message got through. What this story shows is that Daniel's prayers were a covering and a license for the angels to conduct this spiritual warfare.

Our church recently conducted a crusade in Monrovia, Liberia, west Africa, and we noticed a dramatic difference between witnessing there and in our own city. We felt that the demon spirits over the African country had been literally wounded to the point of being ineffective, which gave us much spiritual freedom.

2. **Cities.** Strongholds over cities are especially distinctive in the major metropolitan areas of the world. Have you ever wondered why some of the most famous cities of the world, such as San Francisco and Paris, are such hotbeds of wickedness? Well, satan doesn't want his name associated with an ugly city. He is going to try to

promote his sin in the most beautiful cities. Many of our great cities have been used as incubators for wickedness and the infection spreads to the smaller surrounding towns.

A stronghold in a city runs parallel with the political and media system of that area. It is a unified thought that runs through the minds of these people that causes them to say things like:

"That's O.K., as long as it doesn't hurt anyone else."

"Everybody's doing it."

"Separation of church and state means you can't pray here."

"Censorship!"

You can't effect changes in your city by presenting good arguments but only by binding the strongman and letting God fight your battle.

3. **Races.** Satan has built strongholds that run through the subconscious thoughts of nationalities and races. These thoughts can manipulate people into certain lifestyles

that they may not even desire to take part in. Some of the more common strongholds are:

"I'm German and we love to drink."

"I'm Irish and a temper is just a part of my nature."

"I'm English and I'm just not emotional."

"I'm black and I'm better at sports than education."

"I'm Jewish and I can't be a Christian."These fortresses are lies and they come from the father of liars. Perceptive parents and leaders have become aware of these strongholds and have learned that they can be broken. The only effective way to bring them down is through prayer. A good example of this is the nation of Korea.

For years the Korean people were convinced that they were less than second-class citizens. They were constantly being overthrown by China and Japan. In World War II Japan so demoralized the nation that they burnt all records of the Korean language and refused to allow anyone to speak their

Dr. Mackintosh does not believe in spiritual warfare.

native tongue. This was an attempt to wipe their race from the face of the earth. This and other atrocities built a stronghold of thinking in the Korean people that seemed almost insurmountable.

The Christians of Korea began to conduct spiritual warfare against this type of thinking. Every church from Pentecostal to Presbyterian began 6:00 A.M. prayer meetings until nearly one-third of the entire nation now prays to Jesus an hour a day! The largest and most visible of these many churches is Paul Yongi Cho's church, in Seoul, Korea. The last time I was there visiting his mother-in-law, Ja Cha Choi, I witnessed every night over 2,000 people praying all night long and on Friday night over 35,000 people were praying.

Rev. Cho's church, which recently has over 600,000 members, is not the only large church in that city. Mother Choi's son pastors a church that is running over 10,000. The First Presbyterian congregation has over 75,000 members. As you can see, the Korean revival is rampant. But let's look at what all of this prayer has done to the stronghold I mentioned previously, in the Korean peoples' minds.

In 1958 South Korea was a ravished nation because of the Korean War. Their economy was nearly destroyed and the national morale was the lowest it had ever been. Today this same race of people has become an international industrial giant. Their Hundai automobile has been outselling cars of Japan, Germany and the United States. They are the only serious world-wide competitor to Japan for consumer electronics such as VCR's. How could such a demoralized nationality change so quickly? The strongman has been broken!

4. **Families.** This stronghold can sometimes run through many generations and is manifested with thinking such as:

"Dad was an alcoholic; I'm going to be one."

"Mom screamed at the kids so I'm going to do the same."

"Mother did all right on welfare so I'll use the system, too."

I counseled with a young man once who had felt the conviction of the Lord because He had faked an injury on the job and was expecting to get a twenty thousand dollar payment from the insurance company. He then confided in me that this was not the first time he had done this. I gave him counsel and thought nothing more of it.

A few months later I just happened to ask him where his father was. He told me he was home suffering from a back injury. This aroused my curiosity so I questioned him further. He told me his father had done this for years~faking injuries on the job and collecting unemployment and insurance settlements!

This was a stronghold that was running through his family. I instructed him to pray against it and break its hold and he agreed he would. Unfortunately this young man later backslid and fell away from God. At the writing of this book he is at home, "suffering from a new injury at work."

As I was growing up I noticed strongholds, bad habits, in my own family tree. I later shared these with my wife and we bound together as a family to stop them at my generation. I ask you to do the same. Do not let these kinds of patterns continue.

5. **Personal.** In this area of thinking satan has tried to develop negative patterns since you were a little boy or girl. Sometimes it was reinforced by parents calling you "Stupid," or saying, "You always cry." Many times they are formed by an adult molesting a child or beating him unmercifully.

Sometimes a stronghold can be built by the person himself yielding to the thoughts of satan, like:

"I always have bad luck."

"I'm always late."

"I'm so ugly."

"No one ever listens to me."

These thoughts are very dangerous and can destroy your self-esteem and cause you to constantly live in a negative mental framework. Paul tells us, in Philippians, how to control our thinking:

"Whatever things are true, whatever things are noble, whatever things are just, whatever things are pure, whatever things are lovely, whatever things are of good report, if there is any virtue and if there is anything praiseworthy ~meditate on these things".[85]

Each one of these strongholds that I mentioned are governed by principalities and powers and spiritual wickedness in high places. These spirits nurture attitudes and thoughts through any means possible. One common medium is television. Sitcoms cast actors into predetermined roles that reinforce wicked habits and thoughts in families, races, cities and nations.

News reports emphasize one negative aspect of a city and the whole world thinks that is characteristic of all the people who live there. San Francisco is a prime example of this. Our city's homosexual population is very tiny. They live in two small

---

[85] Phlippians 4:8

neighborhoods, Castro and Polk Street. Because their activity is so bizarre, however, the news media blows it out of proportion, reinforcing the stronghold of thoughts in the minds of the people of San Francisco until they begin to believe that homosexuality is a normal lifestyle.

This stronghold became so ingrained that in November of 1989 the City was ready to pass a bill that would legalize homosexual relationships and enable them for a small fee of $35.00 to have the full rights of married couples!

The Christians of San Franciso immediately began to conduct prayer warfare. The church that I pastor called 4:00 a.m., 6:00 a.m., 8:30 a.m., 6:00 p.m. and 8:00 p.m. prayer meetings. We also had all-night prayer vigils. Three weeks before the election, on a Monday morning, God told me to take our 6:00 a.m. prayer meeting group underneath the Bay Bridge and ask God to "shake" the city. One week later God shook San Francisco with a 7.1 earthquake that was so severe part of the bridge collapsed!

That earthquake was God's way of responding to prayer warfare. We immediately saw a change in the thinking and attitude of our city and the homosexual bill (domestic partnership law) was defeated.

HOW TO CONDUCT PRAYER WARFARE

Paul told us, "...though we walk in the flesh, we do not war according to the flesh. For the weapons of our warfare are not carnal but mighty in God for pulling down strongholds, casting down arguments and every high thing that exalts itself against the knowledge of God, bringing every thought into captivity to the obedience of Christ, and being ready to punish all disobedience when your obedience is fulfilled."[86]

Our warfare must cast down arguments and bring thoughts into captivity to the obedience of Christ. Many people have

---

[86] 2 Corinthians 10:3-6

asked me, "How do I conduct warfare?" First, let me tell you what "not" to do.

1. It is not marching through the streets carrying placards.

2. It is not putting together a voting block and ferrying people to the polls. Jesus said, "If My kingdom was of this world, then My servants would fight."[87] In Roman times you voted with a sword. Though I feel Christians should exercise their right to vote, the church is not a place to conduct a campaign.

3. It is not preaching on the street corner, though at times there is nothing wrong with this. Jesus said to pray in secret and He would "reward you openly."[88] If you are not careful, your preaching at public forums could reinforce some strongholds in peoples' minds that "Christians are crazy."

4. It is not running with a torch through your city. This seems to be a very popular Christian activity lately. I don't know what

---

87 John 18:36
88 Matthew 6:6

an Olympic torch has to do with spiritual warfare. Seriously, do you think satan trembles at the sight of you holding an overgrown matchstick? No! He trembles at the name of Jesus!

5. It is not just printing and publishing tracts and magazines, though these are good activities to be used in conjunction with prayer, for it encourages the Christian community in general. But we are not going to destroy satan's society by stuffing paper down its throat.

6. It is not just running radio and television stations, though this is also good. The fact that they exist does not destroy satan's kingdom. If these media tools were to be used properly they could lead the church into spiritual warfare, but even then it would only be a tool for guidance, and not the battle itself.

Spiritual Warfare is done by people, Christians, like yourself. **You** are the only one who can do it, and it happens when you open your mouth and the words come out. All of the previous methods that I discussed are carnal tools, but "the weapons of our warfare are not carnal but mighty in God."[89] They go into operation when your spirit unites with the Holy Ghost and you engage in battle. There are innumerable techniques you can use for performing spiritual warfare. I will list a few of the more effective ones that churches are using today.

UNITED WORSHIP

When a church comes together for a service, instead of going through a ritual of three songs and a sermon, they should join their hearts together and truly worship God. There is a fine line between a song service and a spiritual warfare worship session. Jesus told us that worship is the highest calling, for the greatest commandment is, "You shall love the LORD your God with all your heart, with all your soul, and all your mind."[90]

This is a description of true worship: When your spirit is completely focused on

---

[89] 2 Corinthians 10:4

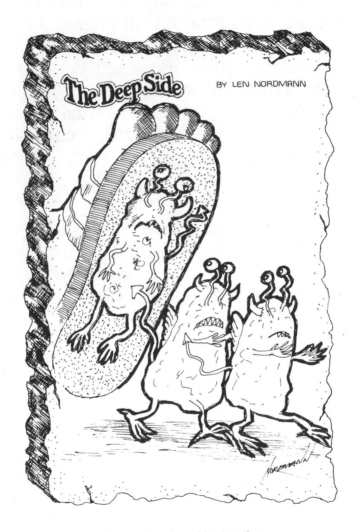

Jesus performing spiritual warfare.

God, your mind has no other thoughts but of the glory of Jesus and your body is centered completely upon adoration to God and desiring to please Him. At this point you are worshiping Him.

Some of the most beautiful songs that have ever been written are now being composed for these types of united meetings of worship. I was recently in England and saw Graham Kendricks lead 60,000 British Christians in musical worship and warfare against the satanic prince of England! After a period of singing they went into a harmonious chorus of singing in other tongues as the Spirit of God gave them utterance. Many Christians received the Holy Ghost for the first time even though theologically they didn't believe it was possible. Now that's breaking strongholds!

In San Francisco I chaired a committee that rented Candlestick Park for the National Day of Prayer, May 3, 1990, for one evening of united worship and warfare. We invited Christians from every denomination to join us. Many told us this was impossible, but with God all things are possible. That night over 5,000 people prayed for the city of San Francisco!

PRAYER MEETINGS

These meetings are conducted by a leader who divides the time spent for prayer into sections, usually ten to fifteen minutes long. Sometimes there'll be music in the background and each section is started off by everyone singing a worship song together.

I have found the most effective way to lead a group of people in prayer is to have an articulate prayer warrior lead the prayer aloud in vocal prayer warfare, while everyone else joins in simultaneously in their own words. While the people are praying individually, they can hear the leader praying in the background. This gives them ideas on what to pray in their own personal way.

This is the method that is most commonly used in Korea. At first I was uncomfortable with it but have since seen its value because of the fervency it brings to the prayer meeting. This method of holding a prayer meeting is gaining much wider use and I feel is a sure cure for the funeral-home, quiet-like prayer meetings of the past. Remember, a prayer meeting is supposed to be conducted in such a way that people will feel comfortable proclaiming things out loud like, "I bind you, satan, in Jesus' Name!"

I notice many churches have been afraid of sounding too Pentecostal, which is often characterized by spontaneity, so they have resorted to the repeat-after-me syndrome and now they are sounding liturgical. Prayer should be natural *and* intense. You should feel free to talk to God in the same way you address another person.

Let me warn you, don't let your prayer meetings regress to thought-prayers, for Paul told us, "...with the MOUTH confession is made unto salvation."[91] My wife, Sandy, leads the 8:30 a.m. ladies prayer meeting. At first the ladies would all sit quietly in their

91 Romans 10:10

separate places around the prayer room and "think" their prayers.

Sandy knew if this continued the attendance would soon dwindle for lack of intensity. So, as the leader she forced herself to begin walking around the prayer room praying aloud. After doing this for a few days the other ladies began to catch on and now their meetings are filled with intense, fervent prayer warfare.

PERSONAL PRAYER WARFARE

This warfare is conducted by yourself, sometimes in company with two or three others. It is important for you to bring your Bible along because the group is small and you might want to share encouraging Scriptures with each other. Because the group is not large it can be very mobile.

I conduct one such prayer meeting at 4:00 a.m. in San Francisco and we go to different areas of the city and claim that "territory" for

God. The reason why we do it so early in the morning is that we don't want our prayers to become a public spectacle. Jesus warned us not to pray on the street corners as certain religious rulers did in His day.

Recently we conducted warfare in the North Beach section of San Francisco. On the corner of Broadway and Columbus there is a nightclub called the Condor. On the side of this building is a state of California historical landmark sign identifying this club as the first topless, and bottomless, nightclub in America. We targeted this place for closure and Praise God, within a few months it was shut down!

One morning, while we were in a circle celebrating before the Lord over the nightclub's demise, a young girl walked up to us crying (this was at 5:00 a.m.). She asked us if we were Christians. When we said we were she fell to her knees, confessing that she was a prostitute and in desperate need for a "hit" of crack. She then began calling on the name of Jesus.

After praying with her we took her to the church to the 6:00 a.m. prayer where the sisters began ministering to her needs. Because of this one contact, we have since formed a Prayer and Share Group on Broadway, ministering to the strippers and barkers along the street!

When a small prayer warfare team goes out, such as the one I just mentioned, we use the model of the Lord's prayer against the fig tree. Jesus and His disciples passed by the fig tree and Jesus saw that it was not bearing fruit even though its leaves were green. He then commanded it to wither and it did.

What the team does is literally lay their hands on buildings that are used for wickedness and command them to "wither" and close down. However, you do not want to become too obsessed with cursing the darkness or talking about satan when you pray. I will explain this later.

Jesus told us, "Whatever you bind on earth will be bound in heaven, and whatever you loose on earth will be loosed in

Heaven."[92] Paul said, "...the spiritual is not first, but the natural, and afterward the spiritual."[93] When you are praying in a small group you are literally mapping out spiritual territories in the "natural". Heaven looks down and sees your strategy and begins to bind principalities and powers around that area.

If you are consistent in your prayer and fasting, after a period of time (that can only be determined by the war in the heavenlies), the area that you're praying for will experience complete freedom from satan's influences. I know many who have done this around their workplaces and have seen many people come to God!

A pastor from Idaho called me early one morning and desperately asked me to pray for a man in his church who had become a political football between two governmental agencies concerning a wiretap. This man was needed in their church and was facing a sentence of forty-five years of imprisonment.

---

[92] Matthew 16:19
[93] 1 Corinthians 15:46

Not only had this man not done anything wrong, but he was becoming the scapegoat for some high government official. The pastor knew only God could work a miracle in his situation.

The reason he called me, was that the judge for the ninth circuit court of appeals presided in our Federal Building downtown. He informed me that the decision was to be handed down that day. At our prayer meeting we formed a team that went down to the Federal Building and prayed a territorial invocation around the building.

At this point I am going to have to use my imagination. I believe as our saints prayed around the building God set up angelic centurions to stop demons from having access to the magistrates that day. When it came time for the judge to cross the threshhold of the building, a big nine-foot tall angel grabbed the demon that was sitting on the judge, back-slammed him to the marble floor and placed his foot on his gnarly neck and simply said, "You don't go to work today." I envisioned that this is what must have happened because that judge dramatically overturned the previous court's decision and set this man free. His release was so unusual it was reported in USA Today, a popular national newspaper.

Sometimes it is not possible for you to actually go to the location where spiritual warfare needs to be made. Pray anyhow; God can take care of the logistics.

WHAT DO I SAY WHEN I PRAY?

I need to warn you not to become too focused on satan. Don't turn your prayer meetings into satan-bashing sessions. I have seen people center so much on the negative that they become that way in their spirits. You don't get rid of darkness by yelling at it, but by simply turning on the light. And, Jesus is the light of the world.

Let me prove this by Scripture. David said, "Let the high praises of God be in their mouth, and a two-edged sword in their hand, to execute vengeance on the nations, and punishments on the peoples; to bind their kings with chains, and their nobles with fetters of iron; to execute on them the written judgment~this honor have all His saints. Praise the Lord!"[94]

You don't need to try to insult the devil and get into a name-calling session. Jude told us, "Michael the archangel, in contending with the devil, when he disputed about the body of Moses, dared not bring against him a reviling accusation, but said, 'The Lord rebuke you!' But these speak evil of whatever they do not know; and whatever they know naturally, like brute beasts, in these things they corrupt themselves."[95] Jude says if we bring a "reviling accusation" against the devil, we will end up corrupting ourselves. Use the glory of God to destroy his power. (This same example is also used in Zechariah, chapter 3).

In a previous chapter we saw how a person might be justified in rebelling but

---

94 Psalm 149:6-9
95 Jude 9

would still be wrong because God hates the spirit of rebellion. The same principle applies here. Though you may despise satan's activities and feel awful things about him, God does not want you to get a spirit of mockery upon you.

This is why many Christians try to conduct spiritual warfare and end up corrupting themselves. In fighting satan they pick up a mocking, hateful spirit which sticks to them and begins to infect their personalities. Before they know it they are no longer bearing the gifts of the spirit ~ love, peace, joy, etc.~ but instead are displaying the works of the flesh, which are hatred, envy, strife, etc.

When I was young I used to study false religions. One day I met some people who are known for their argumentative attitudes. While my sister and I were in the kitchen, we heard the doorbell ring. I answered the door and saw two of these people ready to "witness" to me. I let them talk for a few minutes and then I began to hammer Scriptures at them.

The discussion got so intense that we began to raise our voices until we started calling each other names. I finally shut the door in their faces and marched back to the kitchen and menacingly declared to my sister, "I won"! She looked at me with a knowing look in her eye and said, "Richard you didn't win. You became just like them." Suddenly I realized I could not use satan's tactics to fight his spirits. If I do, he has already won.

You might wonder why praise and worship destroy satan's power. The Scriptures tell us that satanic principalities are ignorant concerning certain things that are common knowledge among saved Christians. Paul put it this way: "We speak the wisdom of God in a mystery, the hidden wisdom which God ordained before the ages for our glory, which none of the rulers of this age knew; for had they known, they would not have crucified the Lord of glory."[96] God wants us to teach these principalities a "thing or two." Paul also wrote to the Ephesian church, to declare "the unsearchable riches of

---

[96] 1 Corinthians 2:7-8

Christk."[97] That all people might see"...what
is the fellowship of the mystery...to the intent
that now the manifold wisdom of God might
be made known by the church to the
principalities and powers in the heavenly
places."[98]

Let me explain this in simple language.
Satan used to be heaven's choir director and
he led worship. As a matter of fact, Ezekiel
said he"...walked back and forth in the midst
of fiery stones."[99] Satan used to live in
worship but when sin was found in him he
was evicted as quick as lightning. When you
begin to worship and praise God, God comes
and inhabits your praises and automatically
satan is expelled.

We need to teach principalities the
manifold wisdom of God. When they do
something bad to you like causing some
sinner to run into your car, they expect you to
get upset and maybe even slip in a few swear
words. But when you jump out of your car

---

[97] Ephesians 3:8
[98] Ibid. 3:9,10
[99] Ezekiel 28:14
[100] 1 Thessalonians 5:17

praising God and run over and show the love of Jesus to the man that just ran into you, principalities are dumbfounded. They can't understand why you would act that way and their power and influence is weakened. In this situation the wisdom that you are declaring is, "in everything give thanks."[100]

CONTROLLING BAD THOUGHTS

CHAPTER 8

Most of us have had the problem of menacing bad thoughts. I have known people who have been so tormented by bad thoughts that they were ready to quit serving God! In this chapter I want to give you a secret that will cure you from having evil thoughts which plague your mind. I also will show you the "glue" that satan uses to make these undesirable surmisings stick to your brain like plaque on your teeth.

THOUGHTS ARE POWERFUL

Many people let their mind run in any direction and probably don't consider what they are thinking about. But thoughts are very powerful. Every building that you see in your town was first created as a thought. The architect put the idea down on paper and the builders followed that plan to complete it.

New inventions and great accomplishments usually don't happen because of great technological breakthroughs, but because someone had a very creative thought or idea. Let me give you an example.

The printing press could have been invented one thousand years before Jesus Christ, because all of the technology that was needed to make it was already available and in use. Guttenburg did not invent something new, he simply took two known technologies that had been around for two thousand years. These were the winepress and the coin press.

Both of these machines were commonly used throughout the Middle East and Europe, but no one had ever thought of combining the two.

In the same way, a positive thought can be very creative and a negative one can be very destructive. The Bible told us that after Judas dipped a piece of bread at the Last Supper, "Satan entered him. Then Jesus said to him, "'What you do, do quickly.'"[101] Here we clearly see that satan has the ability to put bad thoughts in our mind, which can eventuallly lead us down a road of destruction.

Scientists have discovered that the brain remembers things in sequences. Each thought is connected to another thought. This is why when you are listening to a conversation and someone says something that is familiar, it suddenly brings back a story that relates to the topic of the moment.

Scientists have divided our thoughts into two basic categories, or "strings". They are

---

[101] John 13:27

hard and soft thoughts. A hard thought would be the law, and the soft thought would be forgiveness. Now look at the list below and you will understand what we mean by a string of like thoughts:

Hard thoughts	Soft thoughts
Hate	Love
Judgment	Forgiveness
Drafting	Painting
Building	Decorating
Reading	Writing
Criticism	Compliments
Negative	Positive

Have you ever had a conversation with friends and suddenly somebody says something critical or negative about someone else? That comment is then followed by an even worse statement. Before you know it, the conversation is spiraling down to the cynical pit of criticism and gossip and it is very hard to stop. If you do try to halt it, sometimes you are looked upon as a "party pooper."

One time I was on the foreign field visiting a group of missionaries and the conversation suddenly took this downward turn. The ministers at the table began to complain about different people who didn't measure up to their standards. I quickly stood up and excused myself from the table. One of the men became obviously upset at me for this. He asked, "What's wrong Richard, don't you stand up for righteousness?" I replied, "I didn't come all this way to listen to a bunch of negative talk about my brothers. If you want me to speak at the coming revival we are going to drop these conversations." Although they were greatly offended at first, they obliged.

The way our brain works, one negative thought immediately brings on an even worse negative thought and the chain begins forming. From one hard thought to another,

The real reason Esau was late with Isaac's venison.

it will continue until it reaches the pits of depression. Little did I know, there was a pastor sitting at the table who had been so overwhelmed by some of the negative comments that (he confided in me later) he had been contemplating suicide! You must get control over your thoughts and not let them wander in just any direction.

In the previous chapter we saw that your thoughts are really the battleground. It is the mind that satan is fighting to control. You comprehend, through the example of Judas, that satan is capable of placing vile thoughts in your mind. You need to understand that his thoughts are not your thoughts. Even though the mental impression went through your brain, it does not mean you were the originator of it.

Satan has the ability to speak his ideas into your brain. The point that frustrates all of us is this: When do his thoughts become our thoughts? At what point does the "string" of negative thoughts begin?

44444444444444444

THE GLUE

There is a glue that satan uses to make these thoughts stick in your brain and give birth to even worse thoughts. This adhesive is "guilt". As soon as he makes you feel guilty for thoughts that are not even your own he's got you, because then you begin repenting and feeling bad for something you didn't even do!

Let me tell you a parable. There is a man named Joe who had been saved for about six months, whom God had completely delivered from alcohol. One day while he is walking down a street in San Francisco, he looks upon a billboard and sees a picture of a man holding a glass of malt liquor. Satan sees the opportunity and hurls a thought into his mind. "My, wouldn't that glass of alcohol taste good right now?" Remember, this is not Joe's thought. It is a temptation from satan.

Joe feels guilty for having this thought run through his mind and he questions himself, "Why did I think about that?"

Because our brain works in strings of hard and soft thoughts, his mind is soon focusing on the hard string which is full of negative thoughts. After he asks himself this question he immediately remembers the last time he drank alcohol and how good it tasted. These thoughts are now no longer satan's thoughts but Joe's. He's in trouble. It's all downhill unless he knows how to stop this train of thinking.

His next thought is, "Where did I get that last drink?" He remembers it was at a bar around the corner. He says to himself, "Oh no! Maybe I should pass on the other side of the street." Trying to prove he has overcome this temptation, he walks right in front of the bar. As he is standing there satan pours more glue-filled guilt on his brain, *I've already sinned anyhow because of where I'm standing* (notice how satan puts the words in the first person so Joe thinks they are HIS OWN thoughts). *What kind of witness is this, standing in front of a bar? I might as well go in and get a drink. After all, didn't*

Jesus say, if I've done it in my heart I've done it already?"

The suction of self-condemnation works. Joe is overcome with a horrible feeling from even thinking such thoughts! He stumbles into the bar and sees some old familiar faces. He is so ashamed that he runs to the counter and hurriedly gets plastered, to overcome the degrading guilt building up in his mind.

Many of you might be able to relate to this sequence of events. I am sure it has happened to all of us in one form or another~ from overeating to telling little white-lies. Let me tell you how Joe could have easily overcome those bad thoughts...

Joe is once again walking down the street. He looks up at the billboard and sees a man drinking malt liquor. Satan speaks in his mind and says, "Wow! Wouldn't that alcohol taste good right now?"

Joe immediately recognizes this bad thought as satan's. He doesn't feel guilty. He even feels a little amused that satan would try such a silly trick on him. He simply forgets about it and starts praising God for delivering him from alcohol. No problem! There's no temptation because Joe did not accept the "glue" of guilt.

Every one of us has had radical and absurd thoughts pass through our minds, but only the ones we felt guilty for stuck. The other ones pass by without even leaving their addresses.

Jesus had bad thoughts run through His mind! For Paul said, He "was in all points tempted as we are, yet without sin."[102] You see, Jesus had the same kind of evil thoughts come into His mind that you have had, but He refused to accept guilt for them. He realized their source. This is why we are taught to "resist the devil and he will flee."[103] Paul warned us not to give "place to the devil."[104] Do not let him influence any part of your thinking.

---

[102] Hebrews 4:15
[103] James 4:7
[104] Ephesians 4:27

BREAKING THE STRING

If for some reason you have fallen prey to the guilt of satan's thoughts and you find yourself in an uncontrollable situation, let me show you how to bash the sequence of bad thoughts.

James tells us that our tongue is like a rudder that is able to turn a huge ship around. The tongue can turn the whole mind and body towards evil or good. There is thus only one way to turn thoughts to good, even when they are uncontrollably evil. The key is praise. As soon as your lips start praising and worshiping God, your mind becomes instantly clear of darkness.

A brother once walked into my office and the look of depression was all over him as he told me some of the negative thoughts he was thinking. I turned to him and said, "You know what you need to do? You need to stand here in this office and praise God." He looked at me as if I had a screw that was loose. He said, "But I don't feel it."

I told him, "Now that's the most absurd statement I have ever heard in my life. You mean you are supposed to 'feel' something before you can tell Him how great He is? That doesn't sound like praise to me. That sounds like a pay off. 'God, You make me feel good and I will praise You.' No! We should praise God just because He is great and He is who He says He is." The brother weakly said, "Praise the Lord," and then stopped. He said, "I didn't feel anything."

"You're not supposed to. Just keep saying it. It will happen."

After a few minutes of him declaring aloud how good God was, even though he didn't feel it at first, he began to mean it! At that point God did what He said He would do. He inhabited the praises of His people. That brother's mind was soon wiped clean of bad thoughts, and he was basking in the wealth of good positive thinking.

Sister Clara, a wonderful sister in our church, takes what she calls "praise breaks". For one minute during her lunch and coffee breaks she slips into a private area and praises the name of the Lord. It is so effective and refreshing that she has got other employees to join her.

Remember, praise is a weapon, Use it! Don't curse the darkness. Turn on the light.

TRAINING THE SPIRIT-MAN
CHAPTER 9

In this chapter we are going to tackle a very difficult subject. The training of your spirit-man. The reason for this difficulty is that spiritual things cannot be understood through an intelligent explanation alone. It is usually understood only through demonstration.

In high school I had a teacher in shop class who would never allow the students to run the machines. Instead, he taught us about them by using the chalkboard. In the last few weeks of the semester he finally felt we had enough training to allow us to use one of the machines to make spatulas for our parents. When we used the machine we were all thumbs. Two weeks quickly had gone by and only two students out of thirty were able to complete the simple project.

The next semester we had a different shop teacher. Within the first week we were running the machines and by the fourth week every student had completed his first project. By the end of the semester students were bringing home numerous gifts for their parents. The difference between these two teachers was that one taught theory and the other practice.

Paul the apostle believed that "hands on" experience was the only teaching method that should be used by the church~"And my speech and my preaching were not with persuasive words of human wisdom, but in demonstration of the Spirit and of power, that your faith should not be in the wisdom of men but in the power of God."[105] As you and I both know, most of the churches today do not have literal demonstration of the power,

---

[105] I Corinthians 2:4-5

and some Christians have never even seen their first miracle.

The reading of this book, and especially this chapter, will not do you much good if you do not immediately try to put the things I've written into practice. I urge you to step out and put at least one of these principles into action today.

OUR WORLD VIEW

Have you ever wondered why the people in Africa and other Third World countries see so many miracles? The reason is that they have a different "world view" concerning the supernatural. A "world view" is a group of assumptions that have been taught since an early age. Most of us were trained in schools of the Western World. A large portion of people in the Third World never have attended school, and if they did it was probably for a minimal amount of time.

I want us to look at three things that have influenced our world view and how they hinder us from accepting miracles as a normal part of our Christian lives.

1. The assumption that we can know all things. We have been taught in school that if we don't know the reason for something we should at least come up with a theory of why it is that way, which is often based upon limited and incomplete facts. An example of this is Darwin's *theory* of evolution. Since he was not there at creation to view the process, he felt he still had to give an answer for it. With an extremely limited amount of data, namely a vacation to the Galapagos Islands, he invented the philosophy of evolution. Unfortunately, many schools today are teaching this theory as *fact*.

The danger of this method of reasoning is that it does not allow for the unexplainable. People with this world view cannot simply say, "I don't understand it and that settles it!" In their mind everything must be explained, so we are stuck with numerous, incomplete and dangerous explanations that really are just hunches.

When someone is prayed for and is miraculously healed, suddenly questions and speculations arise: "Were they under the doctor's care?" "Could they have been healed anyway?" "Maybe the medicine did it." "Maybe they never had it in the first place."

It is hard for us to just simply accept~ "For My thoughts are not your thoughts, nor are your ways My ways, says the LORD. For as the heavens are higher than the earth, so are My ways higher than your ways, and My thoughts than your thoughts."[106] It is important for each one of us to simply take God at His word, humbly admitting His much greater wisdom.

2. Doubting the supernatural with the rational mind. As little children, after we saw someone pull their first trick on us, we realized that we could be fooled by the sleight of hand. Therefore, built into our thinking is a search for a rational explanation for things that appear supernatural. This thinking is a

---

106 Isaiah 55:8

Moses--Deep thinketh deep.

breeding ground for doubt and causes many people to put more faith in doctors than in God, who created physicians in the first place! It also causes fear to want to move into the realm of the unexplained. A doctor can give you a rational explanation on how he might try to cure you, but someone who prays for you says, "It's faith in God."

I have discovered that both of these world views can be battled by simply choosing to be naive. I have decided that I don't have to know the reason for everything. You must come to this realization, that while you are in this life you are never going to know all of the facts and surely will not be able to rationalize every event.

The study of God's word alone does not bring about miracles in your life. If that were true, our most intelligent Bible colleges would be havens for miracles. While I was visiting Harvard University I was shocked to find that it started out as a Bible school and that their department of theology was still in full swing. When I asked one of the department heads about miracles he looked at me like I had lost my mind and said, "Any so-called miracle that I have ever seen can be rationally explained."

After this conversation I suddenly realized the beauty in being naive. Here was a man purporting to be an expert in the Word of God who smoked, drank and openly practiced homosexuality. He had become so clever ʃ rationalizing that he could justify every siɪ of the flesh. This is why Paul told us not to stray"...from the simplicity that is in Christ."[107]

3. We categorize everything. From first grade, when we learned that one came before two and three came before four, we have learned systems of putting everything into sequences and categories. Everything from training manuals to cookbooks show us how to do things in steps. As long as you follow directions everything is just fine. But the Bible does not fall into these patterns, though we try to interpret it that way. There is no

---

[107] 2 Corinthians 11:3

"seven-step", "four-step" or any systematic approach to salvation listed in the Bible.

The Bible was written in the framework of what is called the oriental mind (the world view of the middle east). This thinking is relationship-based. Salvation is more than just a vehicle to get you to Heaven. It is the developing of a relationship between God and man. When you dated, did somebody give you a manual explaining the four steps to getting a husband or wife? Can you picture a young man dating a girl and carrying a manual with him, checking it periodically to see if he can move on to the next step?

Love cannot be put into nice neat little boxes. Look at these examples. On the day of Pentecost Peter told the Jews to be baptised in the name of Jeus and then they would receive the Holy Ghost. In Samaria we also see they were baptized first and then the apostles came down and laid their hands on them and they received the Holy Ghost. To our western mind it looks like a pattern is developing. You first should be baptized and then receive the Holy Ghost.

Suddenly the whole scheme is blown when Peter is preaching to the household of Cornelius. The Gentiles get the Holy Ghost first and then Peter commands them to get baptized. Did God switch the steps of salvation? No, of course not! There is no exact sequence to salvation. You are saved when you have done all He has commanded you to do. That is why Paul told us to "work out your own salvation with fear and trembling."[108]

I must also say I am not speaking against those who share with people the steps of salvation. I believe it can be very helpful in helping people to get saved. The only danger in this is, when they have completed your steps they might think they're "done", and nothing further is needed.

If you can recognize this desire to categorize, it will help you fight it when it comes to understanding the supernatural.

---

108 Philippians 2:12

Don't allow yourself to say, "Because my experience happened like this, your experience must also happen like mine for it to be genuine." I have heard conversations like this: One person says, "The pastor prayed for me and I got healed." Someone else says, "But my six-year-old daughter prayed for me and I was healed." The first person then replies, "Well honey, I don't know if that's very Scriptural." As you can see, the second woman is told by the first to doubt her experience, based solely upon the first woman's previously predetermined category. I believe God loves to do things out of the ordinary, for the sole purpose of smashing categories.

If you're ever going to move in the realm of the Spirit, get ready for surprises. Sometimes God will just outright shock you. I will never forget the time when my daughter Rocquele, at age 3 1/2, saw me suffering with athlete's foot and walked up in her childlike way, layed her little hands on my feet and prayed, "Zaba zaba booba, in Jesa' Name." The next day my feet were healed.

I'm so glad that God brings surprises. It makes our Christian walk a whole lot more fun, and less predictable.

THE VALUE OF TONGUES

One day while I was praying, the Lord had me read I Corinthians 14:10-11 numerous times: "There are, it may be, so many kinds of languages in the world, and none of them is without significance. Therefore, if I do not know the meaning of the language, I shall be a foreigner to him who speaks, and he who speaks will be a foreigner to me." The Lord told me that many people who have received the gift of the Holy Ghost are foreigners to Him because they do not know the meaning or the reason they are praying in other tongues. This causes them not to pray in tongues often. Also, some Christians feel that tongues is just the initial sign that they received the Holy Ghost, not realizing that there is a beautiful and rich meaning for their continued prayers in tongues.

God then told me to count all of the benefits of praying in other tongues listed in I Corinthians the 14th Chapter. Prior to this time, I only looked at this chapter as a lesson in how tongues and prophecy should be handled when the church is assembled together. I now see that when Paul revealed the power of prophecy, he also was sharing the power of other tongues in one's private prayer time. Let's look at these:

1. <u>V1.</u> You should desire spiritual gifts. Tongues are something to be sought after.

2. <u>V2.</u> When you speak in tongues you are praying in private and other men cannot understand you.

3. <u>V2.</u> You are having a personal conversation with God.

4. <u>V2.</u> No one, not even satan, can understand you.

5. <u>V2.</u> You are speaking mysteries.

6. <u>V4.</u> When you pray in other tongues you are edifying yourself (or strengthening your spirit man).

7. <u>V5.</u> Paul wished every Christian spoke with other tongues.

8. <u>V10.</u> Every person who speaks in tongues communicates with signification (for a good reason).

9. <u>V11.</u> If I understand why I speak in tongues then I will become a friend to the Holy Spirit.

10. <u>V13.</u> If I speak in tongues aloud in the service I can pray and God will give me the interpretation.

11. <u>V14.</u> When I pray in other tongues my spirit is praying (Remember this point; we will talk about it later).

12. <u>V15.</u> Paul confesses that he will pray in the Spirit. You should also make this confession.

13. <u>V15.</u> You can also sing in other tongues. This is called singing in the Spirit.

This is a beautiful experience that many churches around the country are enjoying.

14. <u>V17.</u> When you speak in tongues you do a good job of giving thanks to God.

15. <u>V18.</u> Paul boasted that he spoke in tongues more than every Christian in the Corinthian church.

16. <u>V21.</u> Paul quotes Isaiah, where the prophet told how God would speak to His people using other tongues.

17. <u>V22.</u> Tongues are a sign to an unbeliever.

18. <u>V27.</u> Sometimes God will even allow someone else to interpret what you are saying in tongues.

A sister was once praying in our prayer room in tongues and a woman nearby was able to understand her because she was speaking in Spanish, even though the sister praying had never spoken Spanish before! The woman wrote down the translation and later gave it to the sister. It was very encouraging because it said she had been praying for her mother who had been very ill.

19. <u>V32.</u> When you speak in tongues the Spirit is subject unto you. In other words, you can speak in tongues any time you want to if you have the Holy Ghost.

TONGUES TRAINS THE SPIRIT MAN

In Second Thessalonians, Paul shows us that each of us is made up of a body, a soul and a spirit. "May the God of peace Himself sanctify you completely; and may your whole spirit, soul, and body be preserved blameless at the coming of our Lord Jesus Christ."[109]

We were made in the image of God. Just as God is a Father, a Son and the Holy Spirit so we are a body, soul and spirit. This does not mean there are three Gods, just as you are not three people ("Hear, O Israel: The LORD our God, the LORD is *one*").[110] This means that there are three aspects of you that must

---

109 I Thessalonians 5:23
110 Deuteronomy 6:4

come into perfect unity. Let me explain each one.

YOUR BODY. Your body is your "flesh". The Scriptures tell us that we sin when we are drawn away by the lust of our flesh. Your flesh is always pulling you towards sin. This is the realm of your senses, and is where the root of your adamic nature dwells (the original sin from Adam that is in us). This is the part of us that we want to get under control and, as we all know, it's difficult.

YOUR SOUL. This is your mind, where all of your decisions are made. Some people call it your conscious mind. Whichever it is, it sits between the body and the spirit and chooses to surrender to the desires of one or the other.

YOUR SPIRIT. This is the part of you that is eternal and the only part of your person that can commune with God. Many people have referred to it as the subconscious mind. I personally feel this term is not completely accurate. Your spirit is what leads you in the direction of holiness and

God-likeness. Yielding to the Spirit is the goal of every Christian because it is in your spirit that the Holy Ghost dwells. Paul told us that our "body is the temple of the Holy Spirit."[111]

Your spirit is housed in your natural body but remember, "The natural man does not receive the things of the Spirit of God, for they are foolishness to him; nor can he know them, because they are spiritually discerned."[112] So whenever you are operating in the flesh ~ "It sure would be nice if so-and-so would let me speak"; "If I get that position I'll really be somebody" - you are working against the Spirit.

It is the same problem with your mind. "The carnal mind is enmity against God; for it is not subject to the law of God, nor indeed can be."[113] Your mind has a hard time accepting spiritual truths because, as I said earlier, it seeks to categorize and bring everything down to the level of human

---

111 I Corinthians 6:19
112 I Corinthians 2:14
113 Romans 8:7

understanding, when some things are just beyond it.

This is why when many Christians witness to someone, they feel like they have to tell them *everything* about salvation and Jesus or else the person's blood will be on their hands. They can't understand that it is the Holy Ghost that draws people and that they themselves are just one part of the larger body of Christ.

Many times Christians offend the unsaved because they are trying to dump theology down their throat instead of presenting Jesus. One time our singing group, Richard and the Redeemed, was in Arcadia, California doing a concert at a college. To our dismay only fourteen people came to the event, and all of them were already saved. But we sang our hearts out anyway and shared Jesus with the people.

When we drove the long drive back to San Francisco everyone in the car was somewhat discouraged because we wondered if we had wasted our time, not knowing that we had performed a little part in a much bigger plan. Three months later we found out that there had been two janitors listening in the hallway to our concert that night. They are now saved and board members of a local church!

Don't try to be the Lord's whole body. If you are a hand, operate as one; if you are a foot, do its functions; etc.

YOUR SPIRIT IS SMART

Paul says in Corinthians, "there is a natural body, and there is a spiritual body".[114] Your spiritual body fills the space of your natural body. This is why people who lose limbs experience "phantom pains". I was teaching on this subject once and a man in the audience spoke out and held up his hand that was missing a finger and said, "This morning I woke up and felt a sliver underneath my fingernail. Then I realized I was still missing that finger!"

---

[114] I Corinthians 15:44

When you pray for someone to be healed of a broken arm, for example, what you are doing is telling the natural to come in line with the spiritual arm. "We do not look at the things which are seen, but at the things which are not seen. For the things which are seen are temporary, but the things which are not seen are eternal."[115] When you command a person to be healed, you call "things which do not exist as though they did."[116]

I would like to give you an example of how intelligent your spirit is. I recently read a report comparing the lift-off of the spacecraft Voyager with Joe Montana's performance as a quarterback in the Superbowl. When the Voyager was launched to take pictures of planets across our solar system, scientists could not just point the spacecraft in their general location and hope it would get close enough to get a good picture. They had to make many computations, such as the gravity pull of the earth, sun, and each planet, and how they

---

[115] II Corinthians 4:18
[116] Romans 4:17

would affect the voyager as it flew through our solar system. These calculations were so complicated it took scientists with super computers a long time to make all the estimates correctly. One scientist compared it to shooting a BB through a key hole 1,000 feet away.

Now let's look at the calculations the spirit man is capable of making. The Chronicle newspaper reported that Charles Prevo and John White, physicists at Lawrence Livermore Laboratory, dissected Joe Montana's passes at the Superbowl as if they were physics problems. They discovered there were only two constants that Montana could calculate with on every pass: Gravity and weight; and the shape and size of the ball (and to be perfectly accurate, weight and size change with the temperature). This is a list of the calculations the San Francisco quarterback has to make in the Superbowl in a matter of 2 1/2 seconds, merely to complete *one* pass:

1.   The distance between himself and his target (remember, his target is moving so

he is aiming at a spot that his receiver has not yet reached).

2.   How much force to apply to the ball.

3.   When to release the ball. The ball must not only hit a precise place on the field, but it must arrive at exactly the right time.

4.   The time it should take the ball to reach the receiver.

5.   The rotation on the ball. The tighter the spiral or angular momentum, the faster the ball travels.

6.   The arc of the ball. Montana has to throw it with the right balance of upward and forward thrusts so that gravity pulls it down where he wants it placed.

7.   The drag of the ball. At high altitudes, like Denver, a flying ball encounters less resistance than at ocean level, where San Francisco hosts the Forty-Niners.

8.   The speed of the receiver. Montana has to time his pass so it reaches the receiver at the appropriate time.

9.   The point of release must be high enough so the ball is not batted down.

10. The decision of who his target should be in the first place.   He must simultaneously look out for the running patterns of two or more receivers.

11. How to avoid tacklers, who are running at him with two to three hundred pounds of brute strength, while at the same time concentrating on throwing.

Montana of course, is not aware that all of these calculations are being made by his spirit.   John White said, "That's what sets Joe Montana apart. In order to be cool, you completely turn the left brain off and essentially go into automatic pilot."· All of these calculations sound pretty awesome, but this is what your spirit is capable of doing.

The physicist went on to say that in 2 1/2 seconds a quarterback can make calculations that are equivalent to the ones it took to send

* San Francisco Chronicle, January 1990

the Voyager off to take pictures of the planets in our solar system!

In showing you the intelligence of your spirit, I would also like to show you why it's beneficial for you to allow the Holy Ghost to become your "automatic pilot." If we were playing tennis the same awesome calculations that I mentioned for football would have to be made by your spirit. When tennis players are playing effectively, their minds are quiet and they're in the flow, or "in the groove." When a tennis player is not playing well he might say, "I'm putting on the breaks," "I lost it," "I'm trying too hard," or "I'm listening to distractions." There is a sure way to win against your opponent at tennis, if he'll take the bait. It is the same method that satan uses to mess you up from walking in the Spirit.

If you notice your opponent is playing exceptionally well, ask him to come to the net for a moment and describe why his game is suddenly going so well. If he falls for your ploy he will begin to describe each motion that his arms and feet go through. By analyzing his playing methods he is really beginning to put his body under control of the carnal mind. When you start to play again and he misses a ball, watch his face. He will begin to condemn himself in his mind. This is why the Scripture says, "There is therefore now no condemnation to those who are in Christ Jesus, who do not walk according to the flesh, but according to the Spirit."[117]

What does all of this mean to *you*? Is it all a bunch of technical theory or is there something about walking in the Spirit that you can use every day in your Christian walk? Let me show you how important this is.

The Spirit always looks at a problem as a fresh challenge. The flesh always hunts for an old experience to prove a predetermined outcome. Let me give you an example. I was in St. Louis at a conference when suddenly I felt pain in my side. The pain grew more intense as the day went on. The

[117] Romans 8:1

next day I even considered going to the hospital. However, upon arriving at church I was greatly overjoyed to see that a friend of mine, Bill Sisco,was praying for the sick. Then God told him that someone in the audience was experiencing a pain and needed to receive healing right then. I knew it was me.

I walked to the front and Bill simply said, "Richard, you're healed in the name of Jesus." Instantly the pain left my side and I knew in my spirit I was healed. When I went and sat down however, my carnal mind began searching for old experiences, and sure enough, it found one.

I remembered that a man once told my mother that he thought God had healed him of appendicitis, but actually his appendix burst. Though the pain stopped, giving him a sense of relief, his condition really had worsened. Later the doctors barely saved his life. Now the flesh had something with which to war against my spirit concerning this healing. This battle went on for nearly an hour, even though the pain was gone!

Finally I went on automatic pilot and gave God the glory for my healing. Faith is a spirit and it dwells within your human spirit, and"...whatsoever is not from faith is sin."[118]

The more your spirit is strengthened by the Holy Ghost, the easier it will be for you to overcome the flesh. This will make it easier to witness, worship, give of your substance, pray for the sick, love your enemy, take chances and reach success in every aspect of your life.

One of the best advantages of being Spirit led is that the Spirit overcomes the "judging mind." The "judging mind" is what makes Christians so critical towards people they don't understand, especially if they belong to another denomination. Let me give you a parable that describes this principle.

There once were two Christian men in Florida sitting on a bench early one morning watching the sunrise. Suddenly their tranquility was interrupted by a young woman who was dressed very

[118] Romans 14:23

inappropriately. One man turned to the other and exclaimed, "What is this society coming to? First it was miniskirts, then scant bathing suits and now this! She ought to be arrested."

The other man responded differently. He saw the girl's eyes were closed. He walked over to her and put his coat around her and gently woke her up and sent her back to her home. She had been sleepwalking in her nightclothes.

We can criticize the world all we want, but the reason the ungodly are living in such spiritual decadence is that they are sleepwalking and are waiting for some perceptive Christians to put coats about them and cover their shame.

PRAYER AND YOUR SPIRIT

Many people have told me, "I can't pray for more than an hour because I run out of things to say. What am I to do?" "Do I quote Scriptures or something?" This is where praying in tongues comes into play. It does not take long to praise and worship God and make your requests known. That gives you ample time to pray in the Spirit.

I've talked with men and women who pray more than three hours a day, and most of them say they spend at least two of those hours praying in other tongues. Sister Pauline Parham, daughter of Charles Parham (who led the first Pentecostal outpouring in the United States) said, "The old-timers would often pray in the Holy Ghost for eight hours straight."

We, today, have become too "rational" to allow God this level of control, but at the same time will complain about the lack of miracles in our ministries. It is time for us to get "lost" in the Spirit. It needs to be a common experience for us to be "drunk" in the Holy Ghost.

Recently we escorted a girl home from church who was so drunk she couldn't walk and we literally had to carry her up the stairs. When her unsaved parents saw her, they fell on their knees and acknowledged the presence of God. Let's not be ashamed of a demonstration of the Spirit. What attracted you to come to Jesus? The beautiful church, nice people, clean bathrooms, social standing~or was it the touch of the power of God?

Many have asked me what I think about when I speak in other tongues. Paul said, "My understanding is unfruitful."[119]   You don't think *anything*. Your mind just rests while your spirit prays.

It is like the new automobiles that Detroit assembles. If there was an engine problem with the older cars you usually had to take it to a mechanic who would then have to test it. He would drive it, listen to the engine and generally take apart the car until he figured out what was wrong with it. Today, when your new car acts up you take it to the dealer. They plug your engine into a computer which "talks" to the factory directly and tells you what is wrong with your car.

---

119 I Corinthians 14:14

This is what happens when you pray in the Holy Ghost. Paul asked us, "What man knows the things of a man except the spirit of the man which is in him?"[120] You don't really know yourself. Sometimes you'll have a problem but you can't identify what it is. That's where the Holy Ghost comes in. When you speak in other tongues you plug directly into the Spirit of God, bypassing your own carnal mind, and God begins to transform and correct things that are wrong in your life. Trust Him. He can do a much better job with you than *you* can.

Pastors and saints who are experiencing stress and burnout are having this problem because they won't turn it over to the Spirit. Stop worrying and cast your cares upon Jesus. You'll find it will be so easy to do the work of God when you quit trusting in the arm of flesh. Though I pastor a large church I don't spend my day worrying about pastoral predicaments (and you can just imagine the kind of problems a church in San Francisco might have).

---

[120] Ibid. 2:11

My first and primary call in life is to pray and seek God's face. I find if I will satisfy His Spirit, He will feed my spirit with the wisdom I need to pastor my church, and it takes only a tenth of the time! How can we get behind our pulpits and say we have a message from God when we haven't talked with Him as much as we have talked with our barber?

Give the Lord the sacrifice of your time and let Him train your spirit. "Trying hard" is a questionable virtue. There are thousands of programs and methods to "reach the world", but I believe none of these are going to be effective until you obey the voice of the Lord in your spirit.

I was recently talking with a missionary who was desperately pleading with me to find a program that would bring revival to his country. I told him "*You're* the answer." He replied, "But what am I suppose to do?" I told him he already knew what he needed to have revival. God had already shared it with him in his spirit. He might have forgotten, but the answer was there. After a lengthy thought he replied, "I guess you're right. I've known for a long time that if I really got serious, I would pray three hours a day and fast at least three days a month." The missionary is now doing this and guess what? Revival has started!

God doesn't necessarily need a "program". He needs your total commitment. For each person it is going to be different. I can't give you a prescription for a deeper walk with God. You must listen to God Himself.

If you're to be a leader in the church, people follow what you *do* and not what you say. I was asked to preach at a church on the subject of prayer and the pastor gleefully greeted me. "I'm so glad you are here, because I have been preaching on prayer for the last two months." But after being at his church for three days I noticed that his church *wasn't* praying. I saw very few people in the prayer room. The reason for this was obvious. The pastor didn't pray himself! The only way to lead the people you love to a life of prayer, is to pray.

CHURCH GROWTH
CHAPTER 10

King Solomon said, "There is an evil I have seen under the sun...I have seen servants on horses, while princes walk on the ground like servants."[121] I, too, have seen this evil. This is where Christians who are the "children of the King" live in a society with no respect. Doctors are treated almost like gods, and faith healers like charlatans. It's time that the church takes its rightful place as kings and priests unto the Lord.

The only way you can do this is to bring the masses of people over to the Lord's side. This can only be done through church growth. Church growth is the underlying message throughout the book of Acts. But

---

121 Ecclesiastes 10:5-7

many have asked, "Why doesn't the church grow today as fast as it did during the first century?" The main reason is, we do not use the same methods that the early church did.

Every place in Acts where church growth is mentioned it is connected with some miracle, sign or wonder, except for one instance ~ when Paul preached at Mars Hill in Athens. Then it says,"...*some* men joined him and believed."[122] This is the only time that church growth seemed to be insignificant, and I feel it is because it depended on the spoken word alone and there was not a miraculous move of God connected with it.

In our search for spiritual authority you may ask, "What is this authority good for?" Well this is it! If you have authority with God your faith can cause miracles to happen that will greatly add to the church and destroy the kingdom of satan. When I read the aforementioned Scriptures, I began to desire miracles in our own local church and I knew

---

[122] Acts 17:34

that the only way it could happen would be if I practiced it. I prayed for almost 100 people before the first one got healed!

It was on a Sunday night and one of our associate pastors walked up to me and said he had an extreme case of tonsillitis and needed prayer because the next day he was going into the hospital for an operation. As I reached out to touch his neck the Lord spoke to me, "He is healed." So I simply said, "You're healed." The next day the doctors confirmed this miracle and truthfully, I was just as shocked as they were.

I began teaching in our church that signs and wonders were necessary. The more I taught about it and begin to model it, the more frustrated I became because not too many people were catching on to the idea. They were so used to the old mode of witnessing (hand someone a tract, give them a short run-down on doctrine and invite them to church), that this new idea of working miracles to win people to God was difficult for them to understand.

Then the Lord brought to mind the Scripture in Matthew which says, "A prophet is not without honor except in his own country and his own house."[123] The Lord showed me that one of the things that people were lacking was "honor". They were trying to work miracles around people who had known them for years and consequently did not have a chance to build up their faith by having successes in the realm of miracles. You see, Jesus could not do miracles in His hometown because the people were too familiar with Him. We were facing the same problem in San Francisco.

The Lord gave me the answer, which was to take a large group of our saints to Africa and there work signs and wonders. This African experience would be an on-the-job training miracle school. By the summer of the next year we packed fifty-seven people into a jumbo jet and headed for Africa. When we arrived there we started the day with two

---

[123] Matthew 13:57

hours of prayer in the morning and then a Bible study. The Bible study I taught was simply the great commission that Jesus gave His disciples in Mark the sixth chapter and Luke the tenth chapter, when He commissioned the seventy. Let m e paraphrase both of these commissions and notice how different Jesus' instructions are from the usual way we're taught.

•Don't take any money. You're not going out there to give them food, but to give them Jesus.

•Don't take a lot of extra clothes; be vulnerable. Leave yourself open for God to work some miracles.

•Go visit a house and if someone is open and friendly, heal them. If no one is sick pray a blessing on the house. No matter how evil a house or business may look, bless it anyway. God will decide whether it is worthy or not and will make your blessing return if need be.

•Don't "shoot the breeze" with people on the way. Satan is going to try to get you distracted by having somebody come up and talk about the weather or some other non-important conversation.

•Never argue or fuss, especially on doctrinal issues. You are sent as lambs among wolves. Practice "baa-ing" instead of "woof-ing"!

•Always go in twos or three's; never go alone.

•If someone offers you some food, eat it with no complaints, no matter how sickening it might look or how bad it might smell (by the way, you are protected from deadly things[124]).

•If you are offered a gift accept it.

•If someone does not receive you, don't get angry and don't curse them. Simply clean your shoes on their doorstep. God will see that dusty doorstep and take care of them.

By the way, if you do this satan will "fall like lightning from Heaven."[125]

---

[124] Mark 16:18
[125] Luke 10:18

After we went through these simple instructions I also gave everyone on the African team a little method for praying for the sick, called L.I.F.E.

Listen. Ask the person where it hurts. While they are giving you a description stay sensitive to the Holy Ghost, because many times God will speak to you while they are explaining their problem and He will show you how to pray. There are many ways to hear God speaking to you. Let me share with you a few:

1.You will have a strong thought come into your mind that will reveal something about the person. Sometimes it's just a word. I met a man in England who said he was given the word "brown", while he was listening to a woman describe her problem. Knowing this was the voice of the Lord he blurted out, "The Lord told me to tell you that he loves brown." The statement to him did not make sense but suddenly this woman began to burst into tears, crying uncontrollably!

When she finally finished her emotional display, she explained what had happened. "Ever since I was a little girl my mother dressed me in brown, my room was brown, and my furniture was brown. I began to hate my mother because she loved brown. When you said God loved brown I knew that I would have to forgive my mother."

Sometimes the Lord may give you something that might not make much sense. You'll never know if it's really God unless you speak it out and don't let your ego get in the way. If the person says you're wrong, agree with them. Don't get into an argument about whether you can hear from God or not.

2. You will feel a pain in your body. Many times God will speak to you through a pain you are feeling in your body. One Sunday as I was walking to the pulpit, I felt pain in my right chest. Since I knew it was not the result of some physical problem I had, I assumed it must be from God. I told the congregation there was someone who needed healing in the right side of their chest. When I said those words, the Lord corrected me through a thought in my mind and said it was a woman's right breast. I asked them to raise their hand and receive their healing. A woman had come to church for the very first time because she had just received a diagnosis of having cancer in her right breast. The next week it was confirmed she had been healed!

3. You will see words or a message across someone's face or body. I was counseling with a pastor and in the middle of our conversation I saw the word "homosexual" written across his face. (Just because God reveals something to you doesn't mean you should share it. It might be just for your information so you can minister better.)

I decided to change the conversation and began to share the testimony of a homosexual man who had been saved in our church and now lived a beautiful normal lifestyle, completely free from the stains of the past. Suddenly this pastor began to cry and he said, "You don't know why I am crying, but something has just really touched me." But I did know. God was discerning his problem.

A few months later he met me and made an open confession of his sin and told me how he was on the road to complete restoration. Though he temporarily lost his ministry, he was the happiest man you have ever seen.

There are many other methods of hearing God speak through the gift of prophecy. You need to be sensitive to His voice. Your experience will most likely differ from these, but this is the beauty of prophecy for when a person hears it, "...the secrets of his heart are revealed; and so, falling down on his face, he will worship God and report that God is truly among you."[126]

Intercede. Ask yourself these questions: Why is this person in this condition? Could it be some unconfessed sin or some other problem that is hindering them from receiving their healing?

---

[126] 1 Corinthians 14:25

This is also a time for strong sensitivity. Joyce Chivis, one of the secretaries of this book project, was diagnosed as having breast cancer. She works as an RN at San Francisco Kaiser Hospital, so she knew how serious this could be. One Saturday the Lord showed her that she had not forgiven her ex-husband for how he had treated her. She immediately cried out for forgiveness from the Lord. The next day she was prayed for and God healed her. She has the X-rays to prove it!

To operate in the gift of prophecy, for the Lord to reveal these kinds of things, you need to keep yourself spiritually clean. What I mean by that is: Don't listen to gossip and be a talebearer. This kind of conversation can ruin your spiritual sensitivity. It is cholesterol of the spirit and will clog your spiritual veins which allow the blood of Jesus Christ to flow.

No wonder the Lord would not let the Israelites eat the fat of the sacrifice and David

also said, "Their heart is as fat as grease."[127]
He was speaking of people who gossipped
about him. Remember, your body is the
"temple of the Holy Spirit."[128] One religious
leader told me when you are operating in the
Holy Ghost your body becomes "one" with
the body of Christ (other Christians you may
be praying for). He said it is almost as if
your body is physically plugged into
everyone else's body. If you'll listen during
these times, you'll hear God speaking
through your physical senses regarding needs
that others have.

Fight. Now it's time for the actual
prayer engagement. Have you ever noticed
the prayers of Jesus? They were not flowery
Shakespearian renditions, but instead were
phrases like: "Stretch out your hand", "I
will", "I say to you; arise"; Oh, and I love
this one, "Lazarus, come forth!"

Exhortation. What should the person
do to make sure the healing sticks? The most

---

127 Psalm 119:70
128 1 Corinthians 6:19

common command is "...sin no more."[129] You need to make sure that the person stops doing whatever it was that might have got them into that situation in the first place. And of course, make sure they are saved and a member of a strong church.

After these instructions, I divided our African group into healing teams of three apiece and sent them out to villages to work miracles. Their only advertisement was "healing hands". After the first day we only had two small miracles reported~two small headaches were healed. But by the second day the miracles started pouring in. By the end of the week 110 swollen stomachs were healed, 29 headaches, four blinded eyes opened, two deaf people received hearing, one baby had been brought back from near death...the miracles just went on and on and became too numerous for us to keep up with.

The last night we called a meeting, there were 7,500 people in attendance and over 1,000 received the Holy Ghost. There was

---

[129] John 5:14;8:11

no big name evangelist and none of the hype usually associated with "crusades". It was just average people doing "Jesus stuff".

It is time for you to obey these commands of Jesus. Why don't you just go to the person who lives next door and work a miracle? Or maybe you could go downtown. No matter where you are, you will find people with needs. Reach out and touch their problems with the power that God has placed inside you.

A MESSAGE TO WOMEN
(THAT MEN SHOULD READ)
CHAPTER 11

The best kept secret in the religious world today is the power that women could bring to the church if they were released to minister the way God designed. I have seen many groups of women ministries spring up and become mighty forces for God. I am not so much talking about women in the pulpit (though I heartily approve of this) but women moving in the realms of the Spirit, forming power teams of prayer to break the holds the kingdom of satan has upon the families of the world.

I am not going to present arguments on whether women should be ministers or not. If you don't think they should, you can close the book now, and I hope you have enjoyed everything you have read so far. If you're still reading this book, you're about to comprehend one of the greatest ministries ever unleashed upon this final generation!

MEN NEED YOU

In the Book of Genesis it says, "...God created man in His own image; in the image of God He created him; male and female He created *them*.."[130] This verse alludes to the balance of creation. Male and female were made as "one" rather than as two unrelated people. The next chapter says, "It is not good that man should be alone; I will make him a helper *comparable* to him."[131] Here we get an even deeper insight into the relationship between man and woman. God is saying that man needs a helper and so He created one. You!

---

130 Genesis 1:27
131 Ibid. 2:18

Man experiences weakness when he is apart from a woman. Though he may act like this is not so, it is only a facade. The truth is, he needs her more than she needs him! You women are the balancing forces of our society and you need to understand this. This is why it is so dangerous for a woman to get hung up in watching soap operas all day, trying to support the family on her income alone, or in any other way not reaching her full potential as a woman wielding great influence over her man.

When England discovered the continent of Australia they needed people to work the mines of the country because it was rich in minerals. Since no one wanted to go to this desolate continent, they decided to offer inmates an alternative to prison. They loaded up ships with these male prisoners and sent them to Australia to labor. After a few years, this male society in Australia became very perverse and full of homosexuality. England wondered what they should do.

They finally decided to go to the women's prisons and give the inmates there the same opportunity to move. Within one year of their docking on the shores of the "down under" continent, the society returned to normal.

This conclusion reveals a very important social factor of the desperate need men have for women. I feel women should take part in every aspect of ministry alongside the man, so in every way his ministry is balanced. As a symbol of this, many large churches (including our own) are having their ministers' wives sit on the platform alongside their husbands.

What we are talking about here is not just emblematic. We are talking about a wife being the key to her husband's spiritual success. We find a good example of this in the story of Moses.

After Moses met God at the burning bush and was called to Egypt, he needed to get his family life in order. He first went to his father-in-law and asked for permission to go. After it was granted, he set out towards Egypt. One day they came to an encampment. An angel of the Lord grabbed Moses and sought to kill him! Zipporah, his wife, saw Moses struggling for his life and realized that at any moment this angel would finish him off.

You might ask, "Why was God going to kill Moses?" Moses had shrunk from his responsibility as head of the home and had not yet circumcised his son. This made God angry ~ so angry He was going to murder Moses. It shocks many ministers to find that God is more concerned about them getting their personal family life together than their own "ministry". I have seen too many husbands lose their families while they were building their own "kingdoms". What a waste! Just like Zipporah, you sisters are the key to saving your husband's ministry.

In one moment Zipporah became head of the family because Moses was obviously helpless. She took a sharp stone and cut off the foreskin of her son and threw it at Moses' feet and said, "Surely you are a husband of blood to me."[132] Immediately the angel let Moses go and his ministry was saved.

Once, while visiting a small church, I saw a pastor who was very discouraged because of negative conversations he was having with fellow ministers. I spoke with his wife one evening and shared with her that she was the key to revitalizing his ministry. She took the vision and began having prayer and intercession with the ladies in the church. She then took her husband to conferences that were very positive and faith-building and promoted church growth.

By using her charms of womanhood she motivated him to greatness, instead of sitting passively by while her husband and everything he worked for, died. God is looking for assertive and intelligent women ~not bosses, but ladies who know how to accomplish things without looking like *they* did it.

Moses' sister, Miriam, understood the power of women. After the people of Israel

132 Exodus 4:25

crossed the Red Sea she whipped out her tambourine and in so many words said, "Come on ladies, let's dance!" This was the first time in recorded history the church of God ever had corporate worship, and it was led by a woman.

Women are very vital to public worship in the church. The freedom and sensitivity with which you love the Lord is important for men. Time after time I have seen sisters begin to worship God spontaneously and suddenly the cold shells of machismo on the men begin to break and the "little boys" come out to renew their first love with Jesus.

One time I was in a service where the worship was very mechanical and unemotional. You could tell that all the worship leaders were wondering what was wrong. Finally, the man who was leading worship quit singing and just quietly began playing chords on his guitar, while the congregation waited for something to break the stiffness that was present.

One of the women from the worship team stepped to the microphone and began singing a song of prophesy (a message from God to the congregation) which, in this case, even rhymed and had a sense of verse. Immediately the stiffness broke and people throughout the congregation (which numbered about 5,000), began weeping. Instead of that service being mediocre it became monumental!

The mothering instinct that God gave women has a very essential influence which enables the church to stay healthy. Remember, the church is spoken of in the female gender, i.e. the "bride" of Christ. Consequently, the church is also a mother and is to care for people. A good Biblical example is Rahab the harlot.

When the spies from Joshua's army came into Jericho she protected them and hid them from their enemies. But there was a beautiful motive in her actions, even though by most people's standards she was a wicked woman. Her motherly instincts were as strong as ever. She bargained with the spies to spare her house and all of her family members in it.

My wife Sandy is much more sensitive to the small needs of people than I am. She constantly brings to my attention different areas of the church family that need strengthening. She never does it in a nagging way ("Why don't you do this?", or "Why don't you do that?"), but she approaches the subject as if she is asking for permission to help. It is important not to approach your husband in a condemning way, even though you are more aware of the needs of the family than he is. You must encourage him to fulfill these obligations, rather than boss him.

LADIES

THINK DIFFERENTLY

There is a physical reason why women are more attentive than men to the needs of others. This is because a woman's brain is bilateral and a man's brain is lateral. Let me explain.

Lateral. A man's thinking is compartmentalized. He has the ability to focus on one subject and not let anything interfere with him until a project is completed. This is why, when he comes home from work, he can so easily forget about bad things that happened there. You might ask him, "Honey, how was work today?" He'll probably reply, "Oh, just fine." You'll find yourself having the hardest time getting him to express himself about events that transpired at his job.

The reason for this is that his thinking leans more to the left side of his brain. This is where our center for logic is and why a man makes decisions based more on reasoning than emotion. Many times you desire him to build relationships with your children. You can't understand why it is difficult for him to sit down and just talk to them. The reason is that if a man cannot rationally see the benefit of this kind of conversation, he's not motivated to engage in it. That is why it is important for woman to help set up "logical" situations that are also fertile environments for enhancing father-child conversations. These are: Fishing trips, model building, working in the garden, telling stories or reading books.

Since you know that your husband thinks like this, and you want to motivate him to excellence, it is important to communicate with him while having this understanding in mind. If you know he is interested in mechanical things, include that in potential activities. Sandy has found wisdom in sometimes including a visit to a car lot during our family outings.

Bilateral. A woman uses both sides of her brain. A lot of her thinking leans to the emotional, and is relationship-oriented. When she visits friends she asks about the welfare of their children while her husband asks about their car, job, etc. Women also see more than a man does. When a woman is speaking in front of a crowd it is easy for her to become distracted by one seemingly uninterested person, while a man can narrowly focus on the subject at hand and ignore the distractions in the audience. (Of course, you realize I am speaking generally.)

Being bilateral gives women advantages when it comes to ministries in the church. Since they are much more sensitive to emotions they are usually more understanding and empathetic. Women are many times more open when it comes to the ministry of spiritual gifts so it is important for women not to be intimidated. Allow God to use you in this area.

Pilate's wife was a good example of the sensitivity of women. Pilate was looking at the trial of Jesus as just a case of legal judgment, just another routine indictment. But his wife was sensitive to the immense spiritual ramifications caused by the outcome of this trial. The Scriptures give us a picture of her trying to save Pilate from being the man that sent the Son of God to the cross. She entreated Pilate, "Have nothing to do with that just Man, for I have suffered many things today in a dream because of Him."[133]

---

[133] Mathew 27:19

I wish that every man had a woman who was this alert to spiritual things.

WOMEN SUPPORTED JESUS

In Luke's account of the Gospel he informs us that women paid Jesus' expenses. "Certain women who had been healed of evil spirits and infirmities~Mary called Magdalene, out of whom had come seven demons, and Joanna the wife of Chuza, Herod's steward, and Susanna, and many others who provided for Him from their substance."[134] What a great blessing these women had in using their substance to support the Lord's ministry.

Because women are more sensitive to the needs of others, it is no wonder God uses them to make sure the necessities of his ministry are supplied. The Biblical picture of a virtuous woman is not a passive one, for in Proverbs it says, "She considers a field and buys it; from her profits she plants a

---

[134] Luke 8:2-3

vineyard. She girds herself with strength, and strengthens her arms. She perceives that her merchandise is good, and her lamp does not go out by night."[135] As you can see by these verses, God is expecting women to use these talents He has given them to profit the kingdom of God.

Most of the major ministries today ~ from missionaries to television ~ receive a majority of their donations from women. Though many are donating in the name of their husband, it's the women who see the lack and make sure the money is allocated for it.

If you will read the entire section of Proverbs 31:10-31, you will see that power rests in a woman's ability to run things around the home, that a man cannot mimic or replace. Paul the Apostle saw the need for women to be in the ministry, as he wrote in his letter to the Romans: "I commend to you Phebe our sister, who is a servant of the church in Cenchrea, that you may receive her in the Lord in a manner worthy of the saints,

[135] Proverbs 31:16-18

and assist her in whatever business she has need of you; for indeed she has been a helper of many and of myself also."[136] Paul goes on in this same chapter to thank twelve more women for helping him. Now that's women in the ministry!

Did you know one of the books of the Bible was written to a woman minister? She was head of a church and held a position we would call Pastor today. John the Apostle wrote at the beginning of his second epistle, "To the elect lady and her children whom I love in the truth."[137] He closed the letter, addressing her again. "I hope to come to you and speak face to face, that our joy may be full. The children of your elect sister greet you. Amen."[138] You can see in these verses the affection that John held for her ministry.

136 Romans 16:1-2
137 2 John 1
138 Ibid. 12-13

WARNING: YOU MUST KEEP BUSY

If a woman is not busy working for God and doing the things God called her to do, Paul warns that she will be tempted to do activities that could ultimately destroy the church. Paul warned Timothy, "I desire that the younger widows marry, bear children, manage the house, give no opportunity to the adversary to speak reproachfully."[139] He also warned that if they do not keep busy they will, "...learn to be idle, wandering about from house to house, and not only idle but also gossips and busybodies, saying things which they ought not."[140]

I have seen pastors who have refused to allow women to have authority in the church and suddenly, what would have been their most effective ministers, became talebearers and slanderers. What a tragedy! Don't let this happen to you. Get busy for God! There are many things that women can do. I

---

[139] 1 Timothy 5:14
[140] Ibid. 5:13

cannot give a comprehensive list, but let me just spark you with a few ideas.

1. **Lead a Prayer and Share Group.** Get a group of ladies together at work, home or even school for a time of Bible reading, sharing and praying.

2. **Ladies' prayer meeting.** This is good, especially if you can find a group of sisters who are not working at a secular job, or work later in the day. My wife leads a prayer meeting at 8:30 A.M. every school day. After the ladies drop their children off at school they meet for prayer. A large part of this prayer time is spent praying for needs that are presented by the women attending.

3. **Street witnessing.** This is also effective during the day. Go to public places and look for people who have needs and then minister to them with the gifts of the Spirit. Sandy took a group of ladies to a busy street in San Francisco. They met and asked a woman if she had any needs they could pray for. At first the lady was shocked by the question but soon warmed up and admitted

she was on her way to Texas to be with her son whose mind was "blown" from drugs. The lady said he was crazy and beyond hope.

The sisters from the church began to pray quietly on the street corner, so as not to cause attention to the group. Sandy assured the lady that God was working the miracle. A few days later Sandy received a phone call from Texas from this same lady. She was praising God because the same hour they had prayed on the streets of San Francisco her son's mind was miraculously healed!

4. **Prayer and fasting groups.** Ask other ladies in the church to join you in an extended period of fasting and prayer. There is nothing more powerful than a group of women fasting, to bring power to a church.

Let me share with you a few reasons why fasting is so important. It can be a "cure agency" within itself. Many times when you eat, you may feed a disease that is in your body. Fasting speeds the recovery process up. It also gives our stomach a rest because the food we eat many times causes pressure and releases toxins. Fasting also can dig out root sins of the flesh and also brings most weaknesses under control. Furthermore, I can guarantee that when you fast you will strengthen your spirit. When you cut off eating natural food, you open the door for consumption of spiritual nourishment. Jesus said if we would overcome (fasting), He would give us some of the "hidden manna".[141]

When you fast, you definitely increase your capacity for spiritual food. Remember, as the flesh loses control the spirit gains it. I know a lot of you get headaches when you fast, especially the first couple of days. This is good. Your body is aching because it is cleansing itself of harmful toxins, especially excessive amounts of caffeine. You will find, if you will just press through, fasting will restore youth and vigor to your body.

The Book of Proverbs tells us the reason many people are fat is when they eat too much, it takes sweeter food to satisfy their

---

[141] Revelation 2:17

hunger ~ "a satisfied soul loathes the honeycomb, but to a hungry soul every bitter thing is sweet."[142] Fasting revives the sense of taste to your palate. When you break the fast you will eat healthier foods.

Fasting also breaks food-induced "drunken-like" slumber. Have you ever gone to church on a full stomach and found it hard to stay awake during the sermon? The reason is, when you eat, blood leaves your brain and goes to your stomach to begin digesting it.

You might ask, "Why should I fast?" Jesus did, Moses did and about every other prophet did. You might be intimidated into thinking you can't go on a ten-day fast, but even if you fast one meal I believe it will be profitable.

I used to think that a fast was *total* abstinence from all food and drinks (besides water) or it wasn't valid. I have since come to realize the true meaning of fasting, which is getting the flesh under control. I now feel that even a fast from pleasant breads and

---

142 Proverbs 27:7

meats, such as the one spoken of in Daniel the tenth chapter, can be very effective. Remember, even a small fast breaks flesh control.

Fasting chastens the body and opens the way to spiritual sensitivity. It also breaks food addiction and "habit" hungers. It will humble your soul and put power in your prayers. Jesus taught us that fasting can remove unbelief when He said, "...this kind does not go out except by prayer and fasting."[143]

I have found that a one-day fast begins to restore your mind. A three-day fast can cleanse the carnal mind. A seven-day fast will cleanse your mind and body and gives your spirit total control. Ten days and longer breaks kingdom powers.

Did you know a fast gets you in touch with *reality?* When you deny your body the basic desire for food you suddenly become sensitive to your entire environment, both physical and spiritual.

---

[143] Matthew 17:21

DO IT NOW

The next twenty-four hours are going to tell the difference. If you do not apply some of the principles you have learned from this book NOW, you probably never will. Remember this, action is the key to really reaching spiritual authority. God has called every man and woman to change our world for the kingdom of God. Paul tells us, "There is neither Jew nor Greek, there is neither slave nor free, there is neither male nor female; for you are all one in Christ Jesus."[144] You have no excuse for inactivity.

Someone once asked me how many people did I expect to come to Candlestick Park (which seats 65,000 people) on the National Day of Prayer? I said, "I don't know, but I can guarantee this: There will be five people there: My wife, my three kids, and myself!"

You might ask, "How many do you think are going to seek the deep call of God?"

---

[144] Galatians 3:28

I know *one.*

Richard Gazowsky

Yours in Christ

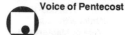

Voice of Pentecost   1970 Ocean Ave.
San Francisco,
California 94127

Ph. (415) 333-1970
Order with your
Visa or MasterCard

MORE

BOOKS & TAPES

Teach Me To Pray
I'm Falling Asleep
By Richard Gazowsky

There is a prayer revolution going on across the whole body of Christ. This book by Richard Gazowsky is a cutting- edge practical guide for Christians everywhere to strike the fire of prayer in their lives. Many have commented on the honesty and the straight- forwardness with which he communicates this message. This book is a "must read" for any Christian who has a desire for prayer. Order two copies and get the third for 1/2 price!

This book, deserves a look:
- **It gives practical prayer methods**
- **It's refreshing in its bluntness**
- **Over 16,000 in print**
- **A real "page turner"**
- **Upbeat steps to effective prayer**
- **ISBN--0-926629-00-X**
- **$5.95, 3 for $14.95**

Teach Me To Pray
I'm Falling Asleep
12-Cassette Series
By Richard Gazowsky

The sequel to Teach Me to Pray cassette tape series, the best selling book by the same title. This completely new material on prayer will unlock any mysteries you still have on the subject. Reverend Gazowsky's teachings reveal how exciting and "natural" prayer can be. A fascinating, revealing, and critical look at how prayer works.

Don't wait, to buy these tapes:
- **The advantage of prayer at dawn**
- **Romance helps your prayer life**
- **How to hear God's voice**
- **Prayer's final battle**
- **And more...**
- **$59.95**

Spiritual Authority
4 Cassette Series
By Richard Gazowsky

This cassette series will make you a "Goliath-stomping" warrior in the Spiritual realm. Full of usable suggestions that are invaluable to the new convert and Bible scholar alike, these tapes will open new horizons regarding the Spiritual ramifications of obedience. Don't let the devil kick sand in your face anymore!

This series, will answer your queries:
- **Defining spiritual authority**
- **The tale of two kings**
- **How to disobey**
- **Steps to power**
- **$19.95**

Deep Calleth Deep Ads

Voice of Pentecost

1970 Ocean Ave.
San Francisco,
California 94127

Ph. (415) 333-1970
Order with your
Visa or MasterCard

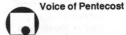

MORE
BOOKS & TAPES

Controlling Bad Thoughts
4-Cassette Series
By Richard Gazowsky

For those of you who are honest enought to admit that you have bad thoughts, help is on the way! These tapes are explosive in their impact, giving down-to-earth, "hands on" solutions to problems that plague all of us. Absolutely a must for even the most righteous person.

These wisely bought, will remove bad thoughts:
- **Battleground of the mind**
- **Secrets to the mind of Christ**
- **Power thoughts**
- **Much, much more!**
- **$19.95**

All About Love
4-Cassette Series
By Richard Gazowsky

It has been said that love is the universal language. Unfortunately many of us have forgotten, or never learned to speak it. This series by Richard Gazowsky deals with Spiritual, and family love. Learn how to communicate with your Maker and your mate.

The greatest of these, is love you see:
- **Falling in love with God**
- **A husband's lesson in love**
- **For women**
- **Did I forget to say "I love you"?**
- **$19.95**

The Healing Seminar
4-Cassette Series
By Richard Gazowsky
The right of every Christian is divine healing from the hand of God! The subject of healing~probably the most misunderstood topic in the Bible~is clarified in this 4-cassette seminar by Richard Gazowsky. Healing is a promise to all New Testament believers, even in these modern times.

Don't be cheated from your spiritual birthright!

These cassettes on reels, will show God heals:
- **A healing model**
- **Making the healing stick**
- **Why does Jesus heal?**
- **$19.95**

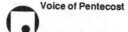

Voice of Pentecost

1970 Ocean Ave.
San Francisco,
California 94127

Ph. (415) 333-1970
Order with your
Visa or MasterCard

MORE

BOOKS & TAPES

Mastering Degrees Of Homemaking
Book By Marilynn Gazowsky

The founder and pastor emeritus of the Voice of Pentecost Church, Sister Marilynn (as she is affectionately called), has recently released her fourth book. Written on the shores of the Caribbean Sea, it is an ideal resource book for any executive-minded, entrepreneurial "manageress of the mansion". With relevant areas for couples and singles alike, it covers topics from architectural accents to world-wide dining.

This tome, needs to be in your home:
- **Making the load easy**
- **Dynamics of dedicated duties**
- **Fun cooking**
- **Tremendous organizing**
- **Really relaxing**
- **ISBN~0-926629-01-8**
- **$6.00**

Teach Me To Budget I'm Falling In Debt
4-Cassette Series
By Marilynn Gazowsky

Do your financial "pockets" seem to have holes in them? Reverend Gazowsky's tape series is a survival guide for those who find themselves needing guidance regarding "modern mammon". A successful real estate investor in the San Francisco Bay Area, she has recently completed the purchase of over $4 million worth of San Francisco real estate.

These cassettes, will ease your debts:
- **Change the mind regarding finances**
- **Percentage breakdown by income**
- **Making wise purchases**
- **Early retirement**
- **$19.95**

Four Seasons
4-CassetteSeries
By Marilynn Gazowsky

Marilynn Gazowsky has done it again! A conference speaker in demand around the world, Reverend Gazowsky's years of Spiritual insights and God-inspired revelations come to light in this series. She shows how a person's life can be divided into four quadrants. An innovative look at the Spiritual transitions that order our lives!

These audios, will put you in the "know":
- **Spring~career/education**
- **Summer~labor and proof of work**
- **Fall~entertaining great people; world travel**
- **Winter~eternal spring**
- **$19.95**

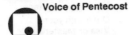

Voice of Pentecost 1970 Ocean Ave.
San Francisco,
California 94127

Ph. (415) 333-1970
Order with your
Visa or MasterCard

MORE
BOOKS & TAPES

Managing Your Time
4-Cassette Series
By Richard Gazowsky

Do you often wish that there were more than 24 hours in a day? Find yourself pulled between business, family and church? In this 4-cassette series by Richard Gazowsky, you'll find the tools to prioritize your time for family, business and your service to God.

Get in line with:
- **Time management**
- **Getting rest in rhythm with life**
- **Getting work in rhythm with life**
- **Getting play in rhythm with life**
- **$19.95**

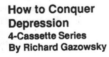

How to Conquer Depression
4-Cassette Series
By Richard Gazowsky

Since the dawn of man, one thing has been common to all~depression. It saps strength, vitality and creativity. Why do some rise above it, while others seem to never become the person God wants them to be? Find the answers and more in this 4-cassette series by Richard Gazowsky.

Reasons why to buy:
- **The environment of faith**
- **Self-talk**
- **Steps to optimism**
- **Goal setting**
- **$19.95**

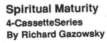

Spiritual Maturity
4-CassetteSeries
By Richard Gazowsky

The lack of emotional growth in a person is embarassing~but the lack of Spiritual maturity is downright depressing! Stop being a Spiritual "cry-baby" and become the man or woman God wants you to be! This 4-cassette series will give you the spiritual "meat" to grow in God.

Follow these along, to make you strong:
- **Becoming of age**
- **Spiritual warfare**
- **Mature Christian women**
- **Mature Christian men**
- **$19.95**

Deep Calleth Deep Ads

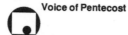

Voice of Pentecost

1970 Ocean Ave.
San Francisco,
California 94127

Ph. (415) 333-1970
Order with your
Visa or MasterCard

ORDER

BOOKS & TAPES

Voice of Pentecost

1970 Ocean Ave.
San Francisco,
California 94127

Ph. (415) 333-1970
Order with your
Visa or MasterCard

Name_____

Address_____

City/State/Zip_____ **Phone**_____

Name of book or tapes you're ordering	Quantity	Price	subtotal
	Sales Tax Add 7 1/4%		
		Total	

Voice of Pentecost

1970 Ocean Ave.
San Francisco,
California 94127

Ph. (415) 333-1970
Order with your
Visa or MasterCard

Name_____

Address_____

City/State/Zip_____ **Phone**_____

Name of book or tapes you're ordering	Quantity	Price	subtotal
	Sales Tax Add 7 1/4%		
		Total	

Voice of Pentecost

1970 Ocean Ave.
San Francisco,
California 94127

Ph. (415) 333-1970
Order with your
Visa or MasterCard

Name_____

Address_____

City/State/Zip_____ **Phone**_____

Name of book or tapes you're ordering	Quantity	Price	subtotal
	Sales Tax Add 7 1/4%		
		Total	

Deep Calleth Deep Ads